Ra by Rail

No. 4 The New Forest

Malcolm S. Trigg

PLATFORM
5

ISBN 1 872524 53 2

© 1993. Malcolm S. Trigg and Platform 5 Publishing Ltd.

Published by Platform 5 Publishing Ltd., Wyvern House, Sark Road, Sheffield, S2 4HG.

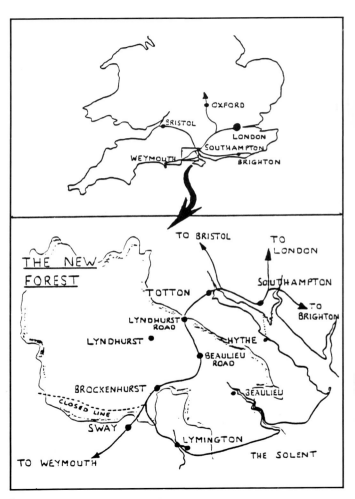

CONTENTS

INTRODUCTION

The New Forest is one of the most beautiful areas in southern England, and in many ways it is quite unique. It has been described as a miraculous survival of Norman England, and in many people's minds it is seen as the last great area of natural landscape in lowland Britain. Like all landscapes however, it bears the marks of centuries of human use, and even now it is a changing landscape as it fulfils many functions. It is a working forest, not an outdoor museum, and it is one of the country's main tourist areas. The New Forest covers approximately 150 square miles and lies in south-west Hampshire between the valleys of the River Avon to the west and the River Test (and Southampton Water) to the east. Its southern edge reaches to the shores of the Solent. The Ordnance Survey map shows the official boundary (the Perambulation) but there is a significant area outside of this which has much of the character of the New Forest and this has now been included in a wider 'Heritage Area'. The electrified railway line from London Waterloo to Weymouth crosses the southern part of the Forest and travellers between Southampton and Bournemouth see something of its varied landscapes. The main line trains are the stylish ''Wessex Electrics'', and one of these is named ''The New Forest'' in recognition of the part they play in the life of the area. While many local residents commute to London the trains can also bring in visitors to the New Forest from a wide area.

A Royal Hunting Forest

The New Forest is not 'new' and it is not all 'forest' in the sense that most people commonly understand this word. It was created by King William 1st in 1079 who set aside this area as a Royal Hunting Forest. The area is one of generally infertile soils and so it has never been farmed very much and has remained a largely natural area of ancient woodlands and heathlands. The many ponies and cattle seen grazing on the Forest are all owned by the commoners (people whose property has the historical rights of grazing attached) and indeed, without the animals constant grazing, the Forest would soon revert to an impenetrable jungle which would destroy its character and prevent easy access for walkers.

A Unique Landscape

Over the centuries the use by the Crown to hunt deer gradually diminished and the Forest took on other roles. About three quarters of the area is still Crown land and by tradition permission is granted for unrestricted access with vast areas over which you can roam at will with only the famous ponies for your company. There are several distinct features that together make up the unique New Forest landscape. Ancient deciduous woodlands are the remains of plantings made to supply timber for the Royal Navy. The heathlands, which are mainly on the higher areas of sandy soils, were formed when woodland was cleared many centuries ago. The fenced inclosures (always spelt with an 'i' in the New Forest) for timber production date mostly from the last century but they contain a wide variety of types and ages of trees and can be very attractive. Open areas of grassland are either natural riverside 'lawns' or areas that were used for crop growing in the last war and then re-seeded to provide extra grazing. Finally there are the bogs which are the result of poor drainage, and whilst being rich in wildlife they should be avoided by walkers.

A National Park?

The Forestry Commission are responsible for the management of the whole of the New Forest (not just the timber inclosures) and this area was one of the first in the country to have a specialist recreation and conservation section to help the Forest cope with the rapidly rising number of visitors. Many other agencies are closely involved with the day to day running of the Forest (e.g. English Nature, the local authorities and the Verderers, an ancient court representing the interests of the commoners) and it was agreed in 1992 to give the area

National Park status with its own tailor made management committee. This is in recognition of its unique nature and the fact that some 8 − 10 million visitors come to the area annually and thus can exert an enormous pressure on it. A major conservation plan was put into effect by the Forestry Commission between 1970 and 1979 and this created car-free areas (most of the open Forest), specially designed car parks, well designed campsites and other interpretive features e.g. way-marked trails (one is featured in a walk in this book). One way to help ease the pressure on the Forest is to come by train and although the railway only crosses the southern part, a number of interesting walks are possible.

Train Services

The stations from which walks are described are Totton, Lyndhurst Road (for Ashurst), Beaulieu Road, Brockenhurst, Lymington Pier and Sway. Totton is now very much a suburb of Southampton but a walk from here takes you into the eastern edge of the Forest. Trains are hourly with extras at peak times and fast through services to and from London Waterloo. Lyndhurst Road serves the village of Ashurst which lies on the official perambulation (boundary) of the Forest, and it has an hourly service. There is an hourly bus service (less frequent on Sundays) to Lyndhurst, the 'capital' of the New Forest. (Wilts & Dorset services 56/56A). One advantage of this station is that you can walk directly from the exit onto the open Forest. This advantage also applies to Beaulieu Road, an isolated halt on the road from Lyndhurst to Beaulieu which is some 4 miles away. There is a pub and hotel by the station and it is a good starting point for many walks. Train services are hourly for much of the day but less frequent in the evenings so you should check carefully before planning a walk. On summer Sundays a limited 'bus service (Hampshire Bus service No. 900) passes the station to and from Beaulieu with its famous National Motor Museum and House owned by Lord Montague. Brockenhurst has been developed as the main rail-head for the

Forest and all trains stop here including the InterCity trains from the Midlands and North. London is only 1 hour and 20 minutes away by fast train and a day trip from Oxford (under 2 hours) would be perfectly feasible. The station is the junction for the Lymington branch (and services to Yarmouth, Isle of Wight) and its services are quite out of proportion to the size of the village. 10 minutes walk from the station will find you in the main street where the Forest animals still roam freely and from there you can go in any direction out into the Forest itself. Sway is the last station on the main line from which Forest Walks are convenient and a 15 minute stroll through this pleasant village will bring you out into the open Forest. Services to this station are generally hourly, with some peak time services to and from London Waterloo. The Lymington branch line provides a very pleasant 10 minute ride through the southern part of the Forest and the town of Lymington with its traditional Saturday market has always been considered a New Forest town although it is now more famous as a yachting centre. From Lymington Pier there is an interesting walk into the remote southern edge of the Forest with the added advantage of views over the Solent to the Isle of Wight. Services on the branch are half-hourly for much of the time and the ride is worth it just to remind you of what a traditional country branch line is like (even if it is in an electric multiple unit!). A number of the walks are from one station to another and there is also an hourly bus service (less frequent on Sundays) on the route Totton — Ashurst — Lyndhurst — Brockenhurst — Lymington which is run by the 'Wilts and Dorset' company (No. 56 and 56A) providing another inter-station link. N.B. In the walks reference is often made to 'up' and 'down' lines in respect to station exits. 'Up' always refers to the line towards London and 'down' refers to the line towards Weymouth.

Walking in the Forest

The most outstanding feature for walkers in the New Forest is that you can literally go almost anywhere you like at will.

You are not restricted to signed footpaths as in most other parts of the country and there are only a few private estates and farms which are not accessible. The whole area is however, criss-crossed by paths and tracks many of which have been used for hundreds of years. Some are well surfaced gravel tracks (including those maintained by the Forestry Commission for timber extraction etc) and others are well worn but at times muddy. Yet others are poorly defined and may be ancient tracks which have largely gone out of regular use. Some are used regularly by animals and their course tends to alter over time. The Ordnance Survey maps show a great network of paths (not 'rights of way' as this only applies on the areas of private land) but things tend to be constantly changing and there is no guarantee that you will be able to definitely find all marked paths. The paths chosen in these walks however, are all clearly defined and well used so you should not find any problem. You will find no signposts (except on the public highway of course). This may seem frustrating to newcomers but it will soon become obvious that they are not practical in such an area and, as there is such a multiplicity of tracks, if you know the general direction you are heading in you will pick up whichever path seems best. You do not have to stick to any path at all but beware bogs and thickets which may force a detour. The walks in this book have been planned for those who do not know the Forest and need the confidence to head out into the 'unknown'. They have been chosen to be interesting and to take you through the most worthwhile landscapes whilst being based on the clearest paths and with landmarks which will not quickly alter. Sketch maps are included with each walk but it is a good idea to have an Ordnance Survey map (the 1:25,000 Leisure Map is ideal) and a compass for added reassurance. It is very unlikely that you will get lost on even the longer walks but if you do, take heart that nowhere in the New Forest is more than 2 miles from a public highway and help is bound to be available there. Unless your walk is entirely on gravel tracks and forest roads you are likely to come across wet and muddy areas, especially after rain and 'Wellington' boots are a good alternative to walking boots. Although so many people come to visit the New Forest each year you will soon find that the majority do not wander far from the security of their cars. Your walks, especially when started from a railway station, will soon lead you into quiet areas where you will meet few people and you can enjoy the peace and beauty of this magnificent Forest.

Watching the Wildlife

One of the most famous sights of the New Forest is that of the Forest ponies which appear 'wild' but in fact they are all owned by the commoners. They should be treated with some caution as they can give a nasty kick or bite if you get too close and it is against the Forest bye-laws to feed them. The Forest has many deer and if you are quiet you stand a good chance of seeing some although they are timid creatures. Travellers through the Forest by train are often able to spot deer grazing by the lineside between Beaulieu Road and Brockenhurst and whilst they are quite used to the passing trains they will quickly bound away when approached on foot unless you are very careful. The woodlands are a wonderful habitat for all manner of mammals and birds and the heathlands support such rarities as the Dartford Warbler and the sand lizard. You may also come across Britain's only poisonous snake — the adder. Usually they will disappear if they hear you coming and trouble is only likely to occur if you accidentally step on one by not looking where you are going. The best advice is to always wear stout footwear and not to walk through the heather away from recognised tracks on a hot sunny day. If you are bitten (and this is very rare) you are advised to get medical advice and if possible to go to one of the big hospitals nearby, such as Southampton General. The Forest is home to a number of rare plants but as always the rule is 'take nothing but photographs, leaving nothing but footprints'. All visitors should follow the country code and show respect for this unique environment.

Enjoying Your Visit

If you can visit the Forest outside the main holiday months of June — September you will be able to walk for miles without seeing another person, and even in the height of summer you will soon find yourself away from the crowds. The Forest is very pleasant in early spring and can be quite magnificent in its autumn colours. You may well want to visit some of the delightful villages as well as the more remote areas of the Forest. Lyndhurst, the 'capital' of the New Forest has an excellent visitor centre and museum where you can find out a great deal more about this fascinating and historical corner of England. There are ample cafes, pubs and shops in this and the other main villages along with hotels if you wish to stay for a bit longer. All the walks contain details of the location of pubs and cafes so that you can plan your walk accordingly. This book has been designed for a variety of people and there is a range of walks from short rambles taking an hour or so, to longer walks taking the best part of the day to accomplish. Some walks can be combined to form a longer route and this should be clear from the maps. As well as forming an introduction to the New Forest these walks have also been designed to incorporate many of the area's most popular tourist attractions. Using the train will help to support the local services and you will also be doing something positive to help the environment by keeping traffic off the already busy roads.

WALK ONE: Approximately 6.5 miles (10 km)

TOTTON TO
LYNDHURST ROAD STATION

*This walk provides an introduction to the New Forest area.
Starting in the urban area of Totton, the first half of the walk
is along quiet country lanes before coming out into the true
open New Forest. The walk continues along well surfaced, level tracks, and passes through a variety of different
landscapes.*

Totton is not at first sight a likely starting point for a walk into
the New Forest, but as a village it had historical links with the
area. For many years it claimed to be 'England's largest
village', but it is now one of the fastest growing towns! Leave
the station on the 'down' side into Station Road and almost immediately turn right into High Street. This was the old village
centre but it is now a 'backwater' almost given over to various
industries. In about 200 yards, turn left at Batts Corner into
Eling Lane. There are still some traditional shops in this area
but the modern town centre is well to the north of the railway
line. Continue along Eling Lane which is a rather uninteresting
residential road but after ½ mile you will find the first surprise

Power From The Tides

At the end of Eling Lane you suddenly come to a delightful
creek full of small yachts which looks out into Southampton
Water. This is Eling Quay and looks at its best when the tide
is fully in. There is a pub (The Anchor) overlooking the unspoilt
quay where once small ships unloaded their cargoes. This area
has a direct link with the New Forest as from medieval times
the village (which is mentioned in the Domesday Book) supplied vast quantities of oak timber needed by the Royal
Dockyard at nearby Portsmouth. In the early years of the 19th
century several small Naval vessels were actually built at

11

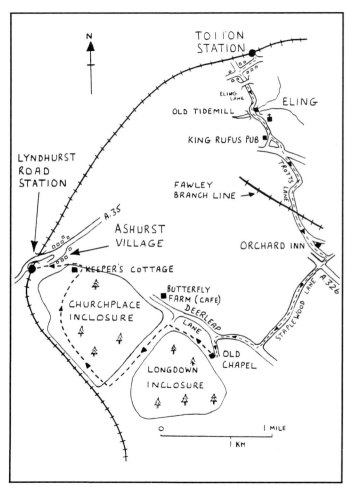

N

TOTTON STATION

ELING LANE

OLD TIDEMILL

ELING

KING RUFUS PUB

LYNDHURST ROAD STATION

FAWLEY BRANCH LINE →

TROTTS LANE

A.35

ASHURST VILLAGE

ORCHARD INN

KEEPER'S COTTAGE

BUTTERFLY FARM (CAFE)

A.326

CHURCHPLACE INCLOSURE

DEERLEAP LANE

STAPLEWOOD LANE

OLD CHAPEL

LONGDOWN INCLOSURE

0   1 MILE

1 KM

12

Eling. You cross the inlet by a causeway which was built to act as a dam to harness the tides to power a mill. The present building was used regularly up to the Second World War and after falling into disuse it was restored to working condition and is now open to the public providing a unique opportunity to see how tidal power works.

King Rufus

The village of Eling is much older than Totton and it is worth while taking some time out of your walk to investigate this interesting and little known location with its church (St. Mary's) which contains an arch built before the Norman invasion of 1066. Continue up the hill past the church and through the old village until the road forks where there are two pubs — The Village Bells and The King Rufus. The latter name is the first real evidence of the New Forest although you are still well outside the modern perambulation. However, this area is closely associated with the Forest despite the cranes of Southampton Docks visible above the trees. Take the left hand lane and you will soon come to a busier road which you cross to follow Trotts Lane, signposted to Pooksgreen. This country lane meanders through farmland and woodland and in about ½ mile you will cross the freight-only branch line to Fawley which transports petroleum products. At the Orchard Inn bear right into Park Lane and in about ¼ mile turn right into Staplewood Lane immediately crossing (with great care!) the busy A326 road. As you meander along this lane the countryside takes on more of the character of the Forest and the noise and bustle of the waterside is gradually left behind.

Deerleap

In about ¾ mile turn right into Deerleap Lane and head towards Colbury. This road can be busy at times but after a short distance it rises and you should take the next turn left up a small lane marked 'No through Road'. This brings you to Longdown, a scattered community of farm cottages overlooking the New

Eling Quay near Totton. This picturesque scene shows the old tide-mill now restored to working condition and which is unique in Britain. The tidal inlet gives access to Southampton Water and in days gone by wooden ships were built using New Forest timber.

Malcolm S. Trigg

Forest. The first building on your right is an old chapel converted into a house and you are now in the open Forest. Turn right by the old chapel and you will soon find a clear track heading north-west with the fence of Longdown inclosure on your left. There are deer in this area but you are most likely to see them at dawn or dusk when the Forest is quiet and they come out into the open to graze. Follow the path for ½ mile until you come to the Forestry Commission car park at Deerleap. At this point you could take a short detour out onto the road where you will see the entrance to the New Forest Butterfly Farm. (see map and Walk 2 for more details).

Churchplace Inclosure

From the car park head south-west across a tract of heathland about 200 yards wide between Longdown Inclosure and Deerleap Inclosure. A meandering track will take you for about 1½ miles, crossing a small stream on the way, until you come to a clump of Scots Pine beyond which is the railway. Before reaching the railway look for a gate into the inclosure on your right. Once through this gate take the left hand fork and follow the gravel track through the inclosure. The map shows the names Deerleap and Churchplace inclosures but in effect it is all one inclosure. The path will take you parallel with the railway through stands of conifers and then into areas of deciduous tress. The sides of the rides are managed to encourage wildlife and in summer this is a good area for butterflies. The path brings you out of the inclosure at Churchplace cottage which is the home of the Forest Keeper for this area. From here the gravel path takes you to Ashurst village in about ½ mile and Lyndhurst Road station is easily reached by a path on your left.

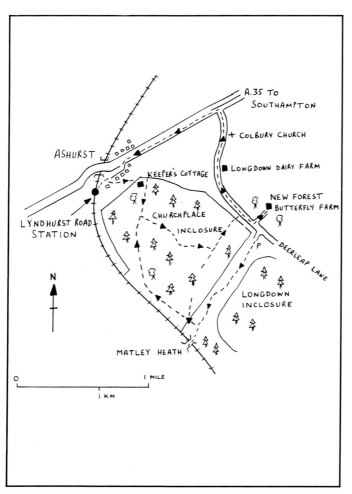

A.35 TO SOUTHAMPTON

ASHURST

KEEPER'S COTTAGE

COLBURY CHURCH

LONGDOWN DAIRY FARM

NEW FOREST
BUTTERFLY FARM

LYNDHURST ROAD
STATION

CHURCHPLACE
INCLOSURE

DEERLEAP LANE

P

N

LONGDOWN
INCLOSURE

MATLEY HEATH

0   1 MILE

1 KM

16

LYNDHURST ROAD STATION TO THE NEW FOREST BUTTERFLY FARM

This walk will take you to one of the New Forest's most popular attractions, the Butterfly Farm at Longdown (open from Easter to the end of October). Walking is easy along gravel tracks through an attractive inclosure and there are two alternative return routes giving a choice of circular walks.

The Happy Cheese

Leave Lyndhurst Road station by the footpath leading directly from the 'down' platform. This path will lead you to the village centre of Ashurst, and as you approach a pub with the delightful name of the 'Happy Cheese' (there was once a cafe on the other side of the main road called 'The Angry Cheese'!) note a gravel path leading to the right of it. This will be your route but first you might care to visit the village and use its facilities. There are several eating places and it provides a pleasant refreshment stop at the start or end of your walk.

Beware of the Cricket!

Returning to the 'Happy Cheese' and the start of the walk, you will see the large building of Ashurst Hospital. The main building was the New Forest Poor Law Institution (workhouse) built in 1836 but is now a hospital for geriatric patients and severely disabled people. Follow the gravel path, passing behind the shops, in a south-easterly direction. The path soon crosses the local cricket pitch and on match days a sign is posted asking walkers to wait for a convenient break in the play before crossing! Until the 1960s the ponies grazed this cricket pitch but when the Forest was fenced this small corner was excluded. After ¼ mile you come to a delightful cottage and small-

17

The New Forest Butterfly Farm at Longdown, near Ashurst. Tropical butterflies fly freely in the heated glasshouses and the site is in a pleasant woodland setting.

Malcolm S. Trigg

holding which is the home of the Forestry Commission Keeper responsible for this part of the Forest known as Ashurst Walk. The Keeper, John Gulliver, is very interested in conservation of wildlife and has done much to increase the butterfly population in recent years in Churchplace inclosure. He is also a recognised expert on hornets although hopefully you will not encounter too many of these on your walks!

Royal Hunting Lodge

Turn right at the cottage to enter Churchplace inclosure and follow the gravel track which takes you through pleasant deciduous woodland. After about ½ mile turn left onto another gravel track. This path winds and rises slightly to pass the site of a Royal Hunting Lodge. Although there are no remains of this, it is a reminder that this was once a Royal hunting forest created by King William I. Nowadays you are quite likely to see Roe or Fallow Deer and although they seem to be getting more used to people, they are basically shy creatures and so you should be quiet if you want to see them.

Deerleap Lane

The path now passes through coniferous plantations and you may see evidence of commercial forestry work. The edges of the paths (usually known as rides) are being cut back to allow more light in and so encourage the growth of vegetation which in turn provides an important habitat for butterflies and other wildlife. After a further ½ mile the gravel path joins another and you turn left, following this for another ½ mile until you leave the inclosure and come out onto a minor road called Deerleap Lane. This road can be quite busy so be careful. Turn right and follow the road for ¼ mile until you come to the Butterfly Farm. The glasshouses contain a lot of splendid tropical butterflies but you can also learn much about the British varieties and so complement your walk. There are good refreshment facilities in a pleasant woodland setting and this is an excellent point to take a break.

A choice of two return walks are given:-

Return Walk (a) Churchplace Inclosure

From the Butterfly Farm turn left and almost immediately right onto a gravel lane leading to a Forestry Commission car park. From the car park follow the path that runs along the edge of Churchplace Inclosure (to your right). The path dips down to cross a small stream and you should then look out for a gate on your right. Before entering the inclosure you might care to go a little further to a bridge over the railway from which there is a pleasant view towards Matley Wood. Returning to the gate, enter Churchplace Inclosure and follow the gravel track which bears to the left and then runs parallel with the railway. You can now follow this for about 1½ miles and it will return you to the Keepers cottage and Ashurst village as on the outward walk.

Return Walk (b)

This alternative walk is along the road, but does allow you to visit another attraction. From the Butterfly Farm, turn right, and taking care, follow Deerleap Lane towards the A35. In about ¾ mile you will reach the 'Longdown Dairy Farm' which allows you to visit and learn about a modern dairy farm. There are also many other animals of interest especially to children. Further along the road you pass the small Parish Church at Colbury before reaching the A35. This is a busy road but there are views to your left of the edge of the Forest and it is a direct route back to the station. There is a bus service if you are really tired by this time, but the distance to the station is just under one mile.

LYNDHURST ROAD
TO LYNDHURST

This walk will take you to the 'capital' of the New Forest. The walk is mostly across heathland, but it crosses the Beaulieu River and there are fine open views. The return can be by bus or could be combined with walk 11 to take you back to the railway at Beaulieu Road or walk 13 to Brockenhurst station.

Leave the station by the main entrance on the 'up' side and walk down to the main A35 road to Lyndhurst. At the station entrance you will pass the New Forest Hotel which provides a variety of refreshments. Just beyond the hotel turn left off the main road into the access road to Ashurst campsite. This is one of the campsites provided by the Forestry Commission as part of the measures to conserve the New Forest. Prior to 1971 you could buy a permit and camp anywhere on the forest but this was leading to increasing problems and so camping was restricted to 12 specially laid out campsites which have proved very popular. Ashurst campsite is open from Easter to the end of October and during this time the site is often filled with caravans and tents. Generally speaking, the visitors do not wander very far from their base and you will soon find yourself well away from any crowds in the Forest.

Mallard Wood

Before the path enters the campsite turn right across an open area of heathland heading south-west. There is no recognised path here but the way is clear with areas of deciduous trees away to both left and right as you cross the heather and grassland. Soon you will come to a small tarmac road which you should cross and carry on in the same direction. The road leads to Ashurst Lodge, an old Forest house now occupied by

21

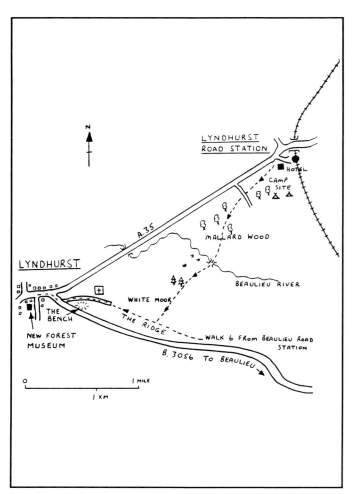

22

a computing firm! Your way now follows a more distinct path but it can be muddy after rain. The path rises slightly and passes through an attractive area of old beech trees on the edge of the heath. This is marked on the map as 'Mallard Wood' although you are not likely to see any mallards until a little further on when the path descends to the Beaulieu river. The heath gives way here to a riverside 'lawn' — the name given in the Forest to grassy areas which are much favoured by the animals for grazing. This area is called Longwater Lawn. The small stream, in which may be seen small trout and other wildlife, is crossed by a bridge and the path continues in the same direction heading for a higher ridge in the distance.

White Moor

The path rises from the river valley to a clump of Scots Pine on Row Hill. To your right is a dense thicket and bog which should be avoided. The path rises and crosses further heathland to reach The Ridge which is the highest point before the Lyndhurst to Beaulieu road is reached. The name 'White Moor' shown on the Ordnance Survey map probably derives from the almost white sandy soil which is clearly visible on the footpaths. This is the result of rainwater washing out the minerals from the sandy soil on which the heathland grows. Where your path reaches The Ridge turn right (North-West) and follow a clear track, now on gravel, towards Lyndhurst. The spire of Lyndhurst church is clearly visible about 1 ¼ miles away and beyond that is the large white shape of Northerwood House. There are extensive views away to the north-east, looking back over the route you have followed, and beyond to the Test Valley.

Bolton's Bench

The path follows a clearly defined route along The Ridge towards Lyndhurst and eventually you will come to the cricket pitch (where the 'square' has to be protected from grazing animals by removable fencing) from where the route is on a

Lyndhurst is the 'capital' of the New Forest. The High Street often crowded with tourists, is over shadowed by the spire of St. Michaels and All Angels Church.

Malcolm S. Trigg

narrow tarmac road. Ahead of you is the small conical hill, topped by yew trees, known as Bolton's Bench. This was named after Lord Bolton, a Lord Warden of the Forest in 1688, and is a prominent local landmark providing pleasant views over the Forest and the village of Lyndhurst. The village, generally recognised as the capital of the New Forest, derives its name from the old English for "Limetree Hill". The village is a meeting point of busy roads and has been the subject of much controversy about a proposed by-pass as the various routes considered pass to a greater or lesser extent across Forest Land.

Alice in Wonderland

The village has a number of points of interest as well as providing all the usual refreshment facilities of a tourist centre. In the village is the New Forest Museum and Visitor Centre which also contains the Tourist Information Centre. This excellent facility provides a good introduction to the area for those who want to know more about its history, wildlife and working life. The parish church of St. Michaels and All Angels has some interesting paintings and in the graveyard is the grave of Alice Hargreaves, nee Liddell, who was used by the author Lewis Carroll as the inspiration for 'Alice in Wonderland'. At the top of the High Street is a very old building, Queen's House, which is now the administrative headquarters of the Forestry Commission. Part of the building is the 14th-century Verderer's Hall where the ancient court still meets every two months to represent the interests of the commoners.

You can return to Lyndhurst Road station on the hourly bus service or this could be used to take you to Brockenhurst. Alternatively, you could make use of the routes in walks 11 or 13 to make a much longer walk back to Beaulieu Road or Brockenhurst stations respectively.

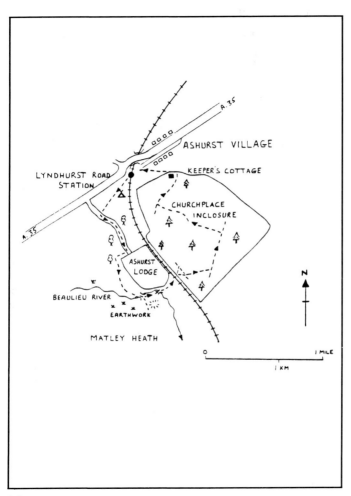

A.35

ASHURST VILLAGE

LYNDHURST ROAD
STATION

KEEPER'S COTTAGE

CHURCHPLACE
INCLOSURE

A.35

ASHURST
LODGE

N

BEAULIEU RIVER

EARTHWORK

MATLEY HEATH

0   1 MILE

1 KM

LYNDHURST ROAD TO ASHURST LODGE AND CHURCHPLACE

A short circular walk that makes a pleasant stroll if you on-ly have a limited time available and want an interesting in-troduction to the various New Forest landscapes. Some sections are along gravel forest roads but there are also sec-tions of the walk that can be muddy after rain.

The first part of this walk is the same as for number 3. From the 'up side' entrance at Lyndhurst Road proceed to the Ashurst campsite and head south-west across the heathland. When you reach the small tarmac road turn left and follow it towards Ashurst Lodge. This road is privately owned and only carries limited traffic to the house and an adjoining farm, so it pro-vides very pleasant walking conditions. The road rises through some splendid deciduous woodlands with mature oak and beech trees under which ponies are often to be found grazing. In about ½ mile the road comes to the entrance of the old house with a clean 'no admittance' sign. Look for a path which turns right and follows the boundary fence, through the woodland and descends to bring you out onto the heath.

Earthworks

You will now have before you a delightful view over the broad valley of the Beaulieu river with heathland stretching to Matley Wood on the southern horizon and the spire of Lyndhurst church just visible to the south-west. The path becomes rather in-distinct, especially after wet weather as it is used a lot by animals, but you should look for a route following the boun-dary fence of Ashurst Lodge and about 100 yards out from it. This path swings round and comes back to the boundary fence at a point where there is a small bridge over the Beaulieu River.

Once over the river turn left and follow the course of the river. If you take a route on slightly higher land away from the river you will find a very clear circular earthwork. This is covered in dense bracken in summer and there are clear signs of animal burrows. Follow the river for about ¼ mile until you come to another bridge which you should cross and this will bring you into an area of old trees with heath to your right. Through the trees to your left is the fence of Home Farm a typical commoner's holding. The farmer lets out beef cattle and donkeys as well as ponies and there is often a large number of animals to be seen in this area.

Stop, Look And Listen!

Follow the edge of the heathland for about 400 yards with the railway ahead of you and look for a small foot crossing which is quite easy to see from a distance because of the red warning signs. Cross the railway with care making sure you close the wicket gates firmly behind you. When the railway was built in 1847 provision had to be made for crossing points for both animals and those who earned their living from the Forest. Between Lyndhurst Road and Beaulieu Road stations there are seven crossing points consisting of over and under bridges as well as this level crossing. Although now only a minor foot crossing this was originally built as a full size level crossing complete with a gate-keepers cottage which survived until the 1960s. This must have been a very lonely spot to live and it is hard to imagine that there was much demand for the crossing gates to be opened. The railway is still a barrier to the deer and the sika deer are only to be found south of the railway.

Deerleap and Churchplace Inclosures

Once safely over the railway take the right hand path that forks away from the crossing and soon you will reach a gravel track. Cross over this to follow another gravel track which gradually rises through coniferous plantations. This is Deerleap inclosure and soon you will be in Churchplace inclosure but the two have long been merged and there is no fence between them. At the next junction of gravel paths turn left and in another 400 yards turn left again. This gravel track meanders through a variety of types of trees and in about   mile turn right, still keeping to the gravel track. This track will soon bring you to the edge of the inclosure at Churchplace Cottage, the home of the Keeper responsible for this area of the Forest known as 'Ashurst Walk'. Turn left here and follow the gravel track which soon brings you into the village of Ashurst with its welcome refreshment facilities and access to Lyndhurst station.

This walk could easily be accomplished in under 2 hours and is a good introduction to the Forest and its varied landscapes for those who want a half-day outing.

A Forestry Commission gravel track in Busketts Inclosure. These tracks are provided for forestry operations but are ideal for walking. *Malcolm S. Trigg*

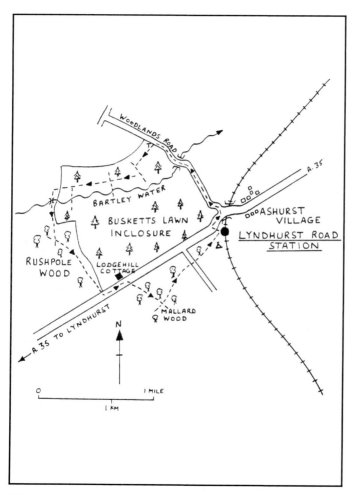

30

LYNDHURST ROAD TO BUSKETTS LAWN

A circular walk starting off along a quiet road and then taking you through a large inclosure to emerge into an area of old woodlands. The walk continues through a mixed landscape of heath and woodland before crossing the A35 (where a bus stop provides a short cut back) and returning across the heathland to the station.

Woodlands

Leave the station by the main 'up-side' entrance, turn right and follow the main A35 as it rises to cross the railway by a bridge. Just before the bridge turn left into Woodlands Road which follows the Forest perambulation with an inclosure on your left and a variety of houses on your right hand side. Along this first stretch of road is a good example of the importance of the ponies to the maintenance of the Forest landscape. Until the 1960s the ponies grazed the strip of grass between the road and the inclosure keeping it closely cropped. When the Forest was fenced and gridded a cattle grid was made about ¾ mile along this road and the ponies were excluded from this area. Since then the grass has become a tangled mass of undergrowth and is evidence of what would happen to the rest of the Forest should the pony population decline for some reason. Whilst the undergrowth is cut occasionally (mainly because of pressure by residents) it is mainly left to encourage a variety of wildlife habitats. Such is the conflict of interests about how the Forest should be managed.

Bartley Water

The road meanders along the Forest edge and just before the cattle grid you cross a small river called Bartley Water. This is one of the few eastward flowing Forest streams and it joins

31

Southampton Water at Eling (see Walk 1). You will cross this stream again later on in the walk. After the river and cattle grid the road rises and on the brow of a small hill you should turn left on a gravel track to enter Busketts Lawn inclosure. This point is about 1 mile from Lyndhurst Road station and in case you are not quite sure of the location there is a telephone kiosk and post box at the point you turn into the inclosure.

Busketts Lawn Inclosure

This is an old inclosure and contains a variety of types and ages of trees. Once off the road and into the inclosure you will soon find the solitude of the Forest although you may meet a few local residents exercising their dogs or out horse-riding. The gravel track leads you at first through an area of young conifers before turning sharp left. In another 50 yards turn right on to another gravel track which you will now follow for about
mile in an almost straight course. The gravel Forest tracks are maintained by the Forestry Commission to allow access for timber extraction and for fire fighting. The danger of fires in these coniferous plantations is high during long dry spells so please be very careful never to discard a cigarette-end or to leave broken glass. At the first 'cross roads' carry straight on but in about ½ mile the gravel track turns sharp left and you should carry straight on along a grass track to the edge of the inclosure which is clearly visible ahead of you.

Rushpole Wood

Leave the inclosure by the gate and then look for a track to your left amongst an area of ancient deciduous woodland. If you are not sure about the path, don't worry, merely follow the inclosure fence keeping about 50 yards away from it and you will soon pick up a suitable track. In a short distance the path crosses the Bartley Water again in a very attractive setting amongst the old woodlands. After the small footbridge you are now very close to the inclosure fence and it is best to actually follow close to this for the next part of the walk. Follow the fence (you can ramble at will within sight of it without risk of getting lost) for about ⅓ mile during which it changes course slightly and then comes to a very distinct right-angled bend. At this point carry straight on in the same direction as the land rises. In a short distance you should find a clear cross-roads of grass tracks on the top of a hill but surrounded by woodland so there is no view to get your directions. Turn left and follow a very clear path in a south-easterly direction. This path takes you through a pleasant area of mixed woodland and patches of heathland and in about ½ mile you will come to the main A35 road.

Mallard Wood

Turn left and follow the pavement alongside the main road for about 100 yards and you will find yourself at Lodgehill Cottage alongside which is a bus stop should you decide to take the easy way back to the station! Assuming you are carrying on walking, cross the road and enter the forest again through a gate and follow a clear path heading south-east. This track takes you through Mallard Wood, a very attractive area of old oak trees, and in ½ mile you will come to a crossing of paths at the edge of heathland. Turn left and the way is now straightforward back towards the station heading north-east. Keep to the path across heathland with areas of woodland on either side. After crossing the small tarmac road to Ashurst Lodge you will soon see ahead of you the campsite, the station and the welcoming site of the New Forest Hotel where you may well wish to find some welcome refreshment!

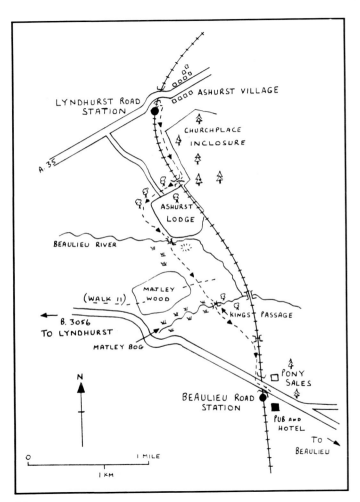

LYNDHURST ROAD STATION

ASHURST VILLAGE

CHURCHPLACE INCLOSURE

A.35

ASHURST LODGE

BEAULIEU RIVER

MATLEY WOOD

(WALK 11)

KINGS PASSAGE

B.3056 TO LYNDHURST

MATLEY BOG

N

BEAULIEU ROAD STATION

PONY SALES

PUB AND HOTEL

TO BEAULIEU

0   1 MILE
    1 KM

34

LYNDHURST ROAD TO
BEAULIEU ROAD STATION

This is an inter-station walk mainly across open country with pleasant views. Most of the paths are rough tracks which can be wet at times and in some places are indistinct. The railway is never very far away, and whilst unobtrusive, provides a useful guide to the route to be followed.

Leave Lyndhurst Road station by the 'down-side' exit and follow the footpath towards Ashurst village. Turn right at the end of this path and immediately turn right again and go through another gate so that you are retracing your route to follow the railway line. Your way is along a broad grassy area between the railway and trees to your left. In a short distance the fence of Churchplace Inclosure is seen to your left. Continue along the strip of grass for about ½ mile as the railway gradually bears left.

A Historical Bridge

At the end of this grass area find a gravel track which rises to cross the railway by a bridge. This is known as Crookhill Bridge and the observant may be able to find an original builder's plate giving its date of construction as 1848, just one year after the opening of the railway across the Forest. The railway at this point passes through dense oak woodlands and it is interesting to think what this area might have been like when the line was built. The track descends from the bridge and passes through the open oak woodlands before rising slightly to bring you to the entrance of Ashurst Lodge. This house was once provided for a Forest official but it is now owned by a computer company. Cross the tarmac road, keeping a straight course, and the path now follows the boundary fence of the old lodge. In a short distance the path turns left and descends through the woods to emerge onto the heath. Keep to the path with the boundary fence still to your left and the way now descends to a small stream which you cross by a wooden bridge.

Signs of Ancient Life

This stream is the infant Beaulieu River and the grassy lawns on either bank are a favourite feeding ground for the Forest animals. Soon after the stream crossing, the path begins to rise on to open heathland. There is clear evidence here of erosion where the path has been turned into a deep gully exposing the underlying sandy strata, on top of which is the thin white sandy soil. This could never have been useful farming land but to your left is a clear circular earthwork showing evidence of pre-historic settlement. A little further on there are some Tumuli, or ancient burial mounds, to your right. The extensive views from this point are very pleasant and you may be able to spot the tall spire of Lyndhurst Church. The path continues over open heathland with Matley Wood to your right. In the middle of the open plain in which you now find yourself, your path crosses another sandy track. Keep straight on but the path now disappears! You are also walking over a very different surface as the land is now short grassland rather than the scrubby heathland you have been crossing. The reason for this abrupt change is not some sudden difference in the underlying geology, but is the result of the second world war. This area is one that was ploughed up for emergency war-time production and was subsequently re-seeded to provide grassland for animal grazing.

King's Passage

Keep on walking in the same direction and ahead of you is a long line of trees that marks Matley Bog through which a small stream flows to join the Beaulieu River. There is only one safe place to cross this bog and if you have continued in a straight line you will come to King's Passage which commemorates the place where Charles II is supposed to have crossed the stream. A gravel track with bridges will see you safely through Matley Bog (which is quite narrow here, but much more prominent upstream) and once through you will find yourself on the edge of another re-seeded area.

A Station with a Pub

These grasslands attract many grazing ponies and cattle, and you should now head south-east across the area towards the far corner where the railway line enters a cutting in the ridge forming the horizon. At this point you will find a clear track which rises onto heathland and runs parallel to the railway (which is hidden in the cutting) for about ½ mile until Beaulieu Road station is reached. The Beaulieu Road pub and hotel is adjacent to the station and provides welcome refreshment at the end of this pleasant walk. This is a remote spot and there is only the hotel and a few railway cottages on the road from Lyndhurst to Beaulieu. Nevertheless, the train will return you to your starting point at Lyndhurst Road (Ashurst) in a mere 4 minutes!

The path from Beaulieu Road Station to Denny Lodge crossing Shatterford bog. Open heathland is typical of much of the New Forest.   *Malcolm S. Trigg*

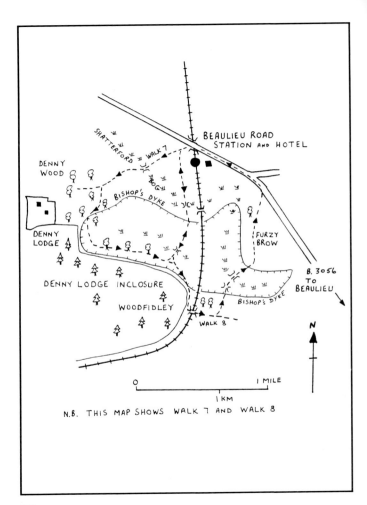

BEAULIEU ROAD
STATION AND HOTEL

DENNY WOOD

SHATTERFORD · WALK 7

BOG

BISHOP'S DYKE

DENNY LODGE

FURZY BROW

DENNY LODGE INCLOSURE

WOODFIDLEY

BISHOP'S DYKE

B. 3056
TO BEAULIEU

WALK 8

N

0   1 MILE

1 KM

N.B. THIS MAP SHOWS WALK 7 AND WALK 8

BEAULIEU ROAD TO WOODFIDLEY

This walk can be combined with walk 8 to make a longer circular walk of 6½ miles as they share a common section (see map). The route is across the open Forest and is mainly over heathland on well defined tracks from which there are extensive views. The walk goes around a large bog and follows in part an ancient earthwork known as Bishop's Dyke.

As you leave the platform at Beaulieu Road turn left on the road to Lyndhurst and at the end of the bridge you will see the Forestry Commission car park and picnic site named Shatterford. The car park is in an attractive clump of Scots Pine and the name refers to the large bog to the west. This area is impossible to cross except by means of the gravel track which you will find heading away from the car park in a south-westerly direction. The path crosses heathland and there is a safe passage across the bog. On the left you should be able to spot the clear outline of some ancient Tumuli and ahead of you are the trees of Denny Wood. This area is popular with bird watchers as some unusual species can be found in this remote and largely inaccessible area of bog and heath. Gradually the heathland gives way to small birch trees which is the natural way that woodland develops. As you enter Denny Wood take the path that turns left to follow the edge of the wood with the open heathland to your left.

Bishop's Dyke

You should soon find yourself on a hill-top amongst some splendid old beech trees, although unfortunately some of these were felled in the great hurricane that swept across southern England in 1987. The view ahead is out over another bog and this low

39

lying area is surrounded by an ancient earth bank and ditch known as Bishop's Dyke which has an interesting history. In 1284 King Edward I granted John de Pontoise, Bishop of Winchester, the ownership of 500 acres of bog and woodland presumably for sport and grazing land for his tenant's cattle. There is a legend that the prelate could only have as much land as he could crawl around on his hands and knees in one day! However, it seems that this theory probably originated in later times because of the existence of the earthworks which could not be properly explained. It seems probable that the area was much better drained when it was first claimed, otherwise its usefulness must be questioned. There has been some drainage in recent times to improve the pasture but it still remains an area to avoid except in following the paths around the edge. The railway cuts straight through the middle on an embankment between Beaulieu Road and Brockenhurst, giving some excellent views.

Woodfidley Rain

The path descends steeply and follows near to the edge of the beech woods for about ½ mile. Where the edge of the woods curve around to the south you should head out over open ground, crossing a stream by a wooden bridge and keeping the edge of the trees to your right. The way now meanders across a variety of heathland and remnants of old woodlands crossing a further bridge as you are at the head of the bog contained within Bishop's Dyke. At quiet times of the day deer are often to be seen grazing on the vegetation in this wet area. As the path begins to rise again onto drier ground you will see the fence of Denny Lodge inclosure on your right which is a useful guide to the way to follow. When an area of conifers appear to your left you should look for a left turn of the path which will take you north-east on a gravel track across Woodfidley Passage. Woodfidley is the name given to the hill behind you (to the south) which is covered in old beechwoods and which is clearly seen from the railway. "Woodfidley Rain" is the local name in this part of the Forest for persistent rain from the south-east. The path across Woodfidley Passage will take you more or less straight back to Beaulieu Road station in a distance of 1 mile, following the course of the railway. This walk is probably one of the most popular with naturalists because of the rich diversity of habitats crossed. It is particularly attractive when the heather is out in summer, but the backcloth of autumn colours in the surrounding woodlands can be very dramatic.

NOTE:

If you want to extend this walk to the longer version carrying on around Bishop's Dyke, do not turn north-east onto the gravel track at Woodfidley Passage, but continue along the edge of the woods with the inclosure on your right. Walk 8 will continue from this point to return you to Beaulieu Road by the longer route.

The pony sales at Beaulieu Road Station. These are held at regular intervals in the autumn and many ponies are sold following a 'drift' or round up. Some are sold for riding ponies and others for horse meat.   *Malcolm S Trigg*

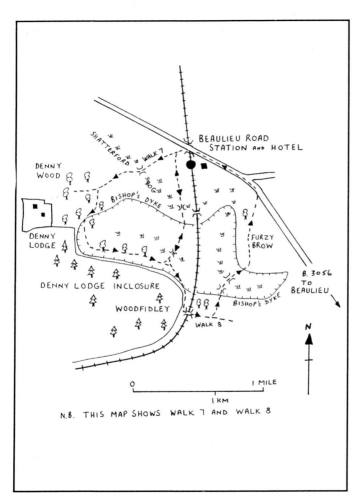

N.B. THIS MAP SHOWS WALK 7 AND WALK 8

42

BEAULIEU ROAD TO BISHOP'S DYKE

This walk takes you around the eastern part of Bishop's Dyke which is described in walk 7. Part of this walk can be combined with walk 7 to produce a longer walk right round the dyke (see map). Most of this walk is over open heathland and there are extensive views from the ridge to the south of the railway.

From the station exit at Beaulieu Road turn left and follow the road down to the Forestry Commission car park at Shatterford. As you walk through the clump of Scots Pine look for a clear track that heads south following the railway which is itself bordered by the same type of trees. The gravel track crosses the Shatterford Bog by a wooden bridge and just beyond this is a small bridge over the railway. Do not cross the railway but continue in the same direction along the path which now is surfaced by almost white sand. About 250 yards beyond the railway bridge the path crosses Bishop's Dyke where the ancient earth bank and ditch is just visible.

Woodfidley Curve

After about one mile you will come to a second bridge over another stream draining from a bog and this is Woodfidley Passage with the woodland of Denny Lodge inclosure ahead of you. This is the point at which walk 7 joins the route, and you should now bear left through open woodland with the heath and bog to your left and the inclosure fence to your right. You are actually following the dyke at this point but it will not be clear. The path rises slightly and bears right around Woodfidley Hill through some lovely old beech trees, still with the inclosure fence on your right. A clear track through the trees soon brings you to a bridge over the railway. It is evident that the railway is on a sharp curve here and in fact it almost turns through 90 degrees necessitating a speed restriction. This goes back to the building of the railway when there was great opposition to it crossing the Forest and the final route was a compromise which took it in a very meandering route. The line became known as 'Castleman's Corkscrew' after the gentlemen who sponsored its building. More details appear in the last chapter of this book. If you hear the trains blowing their horns in this area it is because of the level crossing just round the curve where there are two isolated railway cottages now in private ownership.

Furzy Brow

As you descend the path from the railway bridge look out for the pound at the bottom of the slope. This wooden stockade is one of many scattered throughout the Forest and is used to hold the ponies when they are rounded up in a 'drift'. These drifts are usually held in the autumn so that the young ponies born the previous spring can be branded and some chosen for sale at the Beaulieu Road sales. The pounds are usually located at the end of the open stretches of Forest so that the ponies can be driven in rather like a funnel. The path carries straight on but in about 200 yards you should turn left. Your way is not very clear at this point but you should aim for the end of the line of oak trees and you will soon find yourself crossing the Bishop's Dyke again. A clearer path should now be evident heading for a small wooden bridge. There are two bridges here, and if you are in any doubt, you need the one on the right i.e. the easterly of the two. The path is now quite clear being built up above the surrounding marsh on firm foundations. To the north-east is the high ridge of Furzy Brow and the path up this stands out clearly as it has suffered much erosion. Before you reach this point however, you must cross the bog again, and the path first comes to a bridge by a stream which at this point actually emerges from the mass of grass and moss. This is a pretty spot to linger especially on a hot summer's day, but on no account should you venture anywhere near the bog. It really is very dangerous although it is a marvellous habitat for a great variety of wildlife which can be enjoyed from a safe distance. The path now crosses the bog by a causeway made of old railway sleepers laid end to end. Once over this causeway the path rises steeply to Furzy Brow and half-way up the slope you can cross the bank and ditch of Bishop's Dyke again.

Beaulieu Road Pony Sales

From the top of the ridge there are lovely views over the whole of the Bishop's Dyke area and back to Woodfidley. The name 'furze' is associated with areas of heather and gorse and this ridge is aptly named. Follow the path along the top of the ridge until a small clump of oak trees is reached. This is a pleasant viewpoint and shady spot to stop on a summer's day but you should turn left here and head north-west towards Beaulieu Road. The path descends towards the road heading for a distinct clump of Scots Pine. You reach the road by the end of the great bog called Stephill Bottom. From here it is about ¼ mile along the road to the station and the adjoining pub and hotel. The area used for the pony sales is on the opposite side of the road to the hotel and comprises a series of wooden stockades. The sales are held on the first Thursday of the month during the autumn season and this normally quiet spot takes on the atmosphere of an open-air market with many trade stands as well as the actual pony sales taking place. It is a great occasion for the commoners to meet together and discuss the affairs of Forest life. In this way the old traditions are kept alive and Beaulieu Road has a function, even if the ponies are no longer sent away by rail as they used to be.

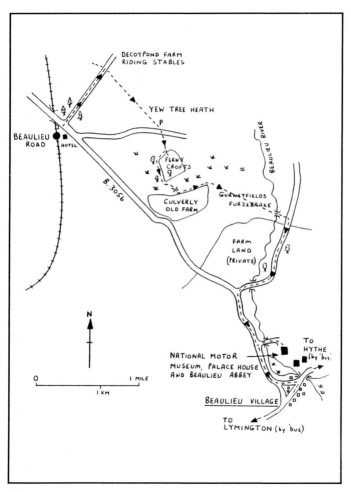

DECOYPOND FARM
RIDING STABLES

YEW TREE HEATH

P

BEAULIEU
ROAD

HOTEL

BEAULIEU RIVER

B.3056

FERNY
CROFTS

CULVERLY
OLD FARM

GURNETFIELDS
FURZEBRAKE

FARM
LAND
(PRIVATE)

N

0   1 MILE

1 KM

NATIONAL MOTOR
MUSEUM, PALACE HOUSE
AND BEAULIEU ABBEY

TO HYTHE
(by 'bus)

BEAULIEU VILLAGE

TO
LYMINGTON (by 'bus)

BEAULIEU ROAD
TO BEAULIEU

You could walk along the road from Beaulieu Road to the village but this is not the best way to see the Forest, and during the busy tourist season it would be quite unpleasant. This walk takes you as far as possible across the open Forest, through some very quiet areas, although the last section has to be along the road as there is no alternative. Beaulieu village is very attractive but the main attraction is of course the world famous National Motor Museum run by Lord Montague. An alternative return route is take the bus to Hythe and thence the ferry to Southampton to regain the rail network, or you could take the bus to Lymington.

As you leave the platform at Beaulieu Road turn right to the pub and hotel. Immediately opposite the hotel is a narrow tarmac road signed to 'riding stables only'. This road leads to Decoy Pond Farm and you should follow this road for about of a mile which takes you out over open heathland.

Yew Tree Heath

As the view opens up to your left look for a rough track which crosses the road. This junction is before the tarmac road starts to descend to the farm and the track you require leads off to the right (south-east) where there is a Forestry Commission car barrier. (These low, single bar gates are common in the Forest and usually bear the inscription 'car-free area'). The path ahead is now straight across a plateau of heather with distant views of the chimneys at Fawley refinery on Southampton Water. This is Yew Tree Heath although there is no sign of any Yew tress now along your way. In about of a mile you will see an Ordnance Survey triangulation pillar (one of those concrete pillars about 5 feet high) to your right and the path comes to a Forestry Commission car park. The short road linking this to the public highway bears the unmistakable surface of war-time concrete bearing witness to the strategic importance of the Forest in times of war. With Southampton Docks just visible, this high point was an excellent location for anti-aircraft guns and an observation point.

Boy Scouts

When you reach the minor road look out for a gravel track almost opposite which is signposted to 'Ferny Crofts-the Scout Centre of Hampshire'. Follow this track until the entrance is seen ahead of you and then follow a clear Forest track leading off through the trees to your right. This path takes a clearly defined route around the edge of 'Ferny Crofts' passing through some very attractive oak and beech woodland, past some small ponds and with open views over heathland to your right. This is a generally quiet area although you may hear something of the various Scout camps at times! The path emerges from the woodland and then descends to cross a bog by means of a causeway and bridge.

Gurnetfields Furzebrake

Once over the bog the path rises again and very soon comes to a fence beyond which is the unusual sight in the Forest of arable farmland. This belongs to Culverly Old Farm and you should turn left and find a meandering track in woodland which follows the farm boundary with the bog to your left. In about ½ mile the end of the farm is reached and the fence turns sharply to the south-east. Your path ends here and you will find yourself on the edge of a long stretch of grassland which is another of the areas re-seeded after war-time use for emergency crop growing. This area has the delightful name of Gurnetfields Furzebrake and it provides easy walking conditions with the added attraction of many grazing animals. This is a long thin area of grassland and you should head south-east towards the far corner keeping quite near to the edge of the heath on your left. An additional landmark is a house amongst the trees on the horizon named appropriately 'The House in the Wood'. About   of a mile of pleasant walking will bring you to a bridge over the Beaulieu River and just beyond is North Gate and the road to Beaulieu. At this point you have no option but to turn right and follow the road as the land beyond is owned by the Beaulieu Estate and there is no public access.

Open Every Day of the Year

In about ½ mile you will come to a junction with the B3056 and you should turn left for a further ½ mile until you see the entrance to the National Motor Museum on your left. A large sign proudly proclaims "Open Every Day of the Year" and it is an imposing entrance to one of the country's leading tourist attractions. As well as the Motor Museum there is Palace House and Beaulieu Abbey all on the same site and reached from the same access. As you would expect from a leading national attraction there is everything you could need for an enjoyable day-out and you could easily spend the best part of a day here. A mono-rail takes you on a spectacular tree top ride around the grounds and the museum has a visitor ride called 'Wheels' which takes you through the history of motoring. The museum building contains one of the world's largest collections of vehicles displayed in attractive settings. During the summer months there are displays of some of the old cars in action but at any season there is much of interest. Palace House is the home of Lord Montague, whose family have lived here since 1538, and it contains a good collection of paintings and furniture. The Abbey was founded in 1204 by King John as a monastery of the Cistercian order. It was destroyed during the Reformation and today only the refectory remains, converted into the parish church, although other ruins may be seen.

Ferries and Trains

If you want a quieter look at the village of Beaulieu carry on along the B3056 for ¼ mile until the splendid view over the large mill pond appears. The Beaulieu River is tidal beyond this point and the river was dammed to power a mill in days gone by. The village is an attractive cluster of old cottages with a large hotel and a small quay on the tidal side of the old mill. You could of course return to Beaulieu Road by retracing your steps but three alternative routes are possible using public transport. A bus service (Wilts and Dorset service 112) operates between Lymington and Hythe via Beaulieu with a short detour to provide a service direct to the Motor Museum. This service is irregular but is approximately every 1½ − 2 hours. An interesting route is to take this service to Hythe, an old Forest village on the west bank of Southampton Water. A regular ferry service operates from here to Southampton Town Quay and an interesting part of the journey is the trip along Hythe Pier in a vintage narrow gauge train! An alternative return trip would be to use the bus service from Beaulieu to Lymington with its ferry service to Yarmouth, Isle of Wight, and use the branch train service back to the main line at Brockenhurst. On summer Sundays and Bank Holidays there is also a special limited bus service which operates between Beaulieu and Beaulieu Road station. This is part of 'Sunda Rider' route 900 from Winchester − Romsey − Beaulieu operated by Hampshire Bus (for details see the information page at the end of this book).

BEAULIEU ROAD - A SHORT CIRCULAR RAMBLE

This is a short ramble over open heathland which could be done in an hour, allowing a pleasant walk between train services if you haven't much time. Alternatively it provides an easy route for a family walk when time doesn't matter. Most of the paths are clear and dry although one section can be wet after heavy rain.

As you leave the platform at Beaulieu Road turn right and proceed to the pub and hotel on your right. Opposite is the small tarmac road leading to Decoy Pond Farm riding stables. Walk along this road for about ½ mile across open heathland until a valley is clear on your left. There is a Forest path which crosses the road and you should turn left to follow this down into the valley with the railway visible in the distance running on an embankment. This section can be muddy after wet weather but the path is clear and heads for a bridge under the railway. Your way is across open heath and to the right a thicket of trees marks the course of the Beaulieu River although access is almost impossible due to the boggy conditions so typical of the Forest streams.

Cattle Creep

The path soon comes to the railway and passes beneath it. When the line was built, access points had to be made at frequent intervals to allow the animals to cross. This route is used now by pony riders as well as the free roaming animals although the deer seem unwilling to make use of the facilities. Similar 'cattle creeps' had to be built when the main roads across the forest were fenced in the 1960s. Once under the railway you will see ahead of you a large open area of grass, which is one of the areas re-seeded after war time use for crop growing. You

51

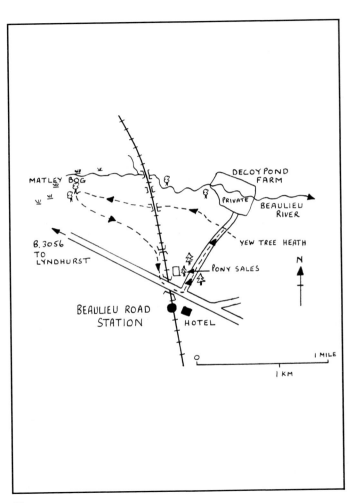

MATLEY BOG

DECOY POND FARM

PRIVATE

BEAULIEU RIVER

YEW TREE HEATH

B.3056 TO LYNDHURST

N

PONY SALES

BEAULIEU ROAD STATION

HOTEL

0   1 MILE
         1 KM

may wander freely over this area but it is best to keep to the left with a heather covered slope rising above you. Follow this edge for ½ mile until at the end of the grassland section you come to a clump of silver birch trees. Amongst these trees you will find a path which doubles back on your route, climbing to your left onto the ridge. This path now leads back towards Beaulieu Road across open heath giving good views in all directions. In about ½ mile the path meets another and you should turn right along this which runs parallel to the railway to return you to the station and hotel.

A typical New Forest scene on the outskirts of Beaulieu village.   *Malcolm S. Trigg*

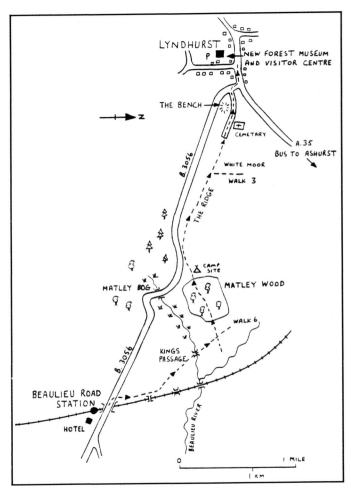

BEAULIEU ROAD TO LYNDHURST

This walk takes in parts of walks 3 and 6 and the maps should be looked at in relation to each other. By careful planning, a series of alternative walks can be worked out e.g. Beaulieu Road – Lyndhurst – Lyndhurst Road. It should be quite easy to follow the routes even when they are in the reverse direction to that described. Walking is easy, along generally dry paths with extensive views over heathland.

From the platform exit at Beaulieu Road turn left and go down the road towards Lyndhurst. At the foot of the road bridge turn right on to a well defined gravel track running parallel with the railway. This first section is the end of walk 6 in reverse and you should follow the path for ¾ mile until a panoramic view opens ahead of you. The railway stretches to your right and your way lies ahead across the wide open grassy plain below.

Matley Bog and Matley Wood

The path descends and finishes on the edge of the grassy plain. You should head out across the middle of this towards a line of trees which marks the course of a stream flowing from Matley Bog. Aim for about half way along this line of trees and you should soon spot the bridge marking the way through the bog known as King's Passage. This is the only safe way across this alder thicket which always causes boggy conditions in the Forest. Once through King's Passage you are once more on a grassy plain, yet another of the re-seeded areas. Keep straight ahead as the land rises until you reach a path at right angles. Here you leave the route of walk 6 and you should turn left here and head south-west towards Matley Wood with Matley Bog away to your left. Matley Wood is a delightful area of old

55

oak and holly trees and you should follow the path straight ahead through the woods. At the top of the hill as you leave the woods you will find yourself in one of the Forestry Commission's campsites. The path goes through the site, which is of course deserted in the winter months, and emerges onto The Ridge. The path comes close to the road (B.3056) for a short while but soon veers away to follow a solitary course along the top of the hill. There are fine views to the east over the valley of the Beaulieu River and you can easily see the route of walk 3 from Lyndhurst Road station to Lyndhurst which you join in about   mile. The rest of the way, and details of Lyndhurst are found in walk 3.

The walk into Lyndhurst takes you past Bolton's Bench. The church spire is visible for many miles around.

Malcolm S. Trigg

BEAULIEU ROAD
TO BROCKENHURST

This inter-station walk takes you through one of the main areas of continuous woodland in the centre of the Forest. Most of the walk is along gravel tracks providing good walking conditions at all times of the year although there are sections where the path is indistinct.

This walk starts off in the same direction as No. 7. From the station exit turn left and go down the road bridge to Shatterford car-park. From here locate the clear footpath heading south-west which crosses the bog called Shatterford Bottom. Ahead of you is the mass of trees of Denny Wood and as you approach the edge of the woods the path for walk 7 turns left. You should now keep straight on into the delightful old woodlands but don't despair if the path seems to fade out. A lot of old paths, even those shown on the Ordnance Survey maps, may not always be easy to find in a forest which is constantly changing.

Denny Lodge

The best advice in this section is to keep straight on until you come to a tarmac road leading to Denny Lodge. Your way is along the top of a ridge and if you sense that you are on falling ground either to left or right, then merely correct your course. The dense trees may distort your sense of direction but you will inevitably reach the tarmac road in under half a mile. Take heart, for once you are on the road, the rest of the way is very straightforward! At whichever point you reach the road turn left and in a short distance you will pass over the brow of a hill and will find yourself in the small settlement of Denny Lodge. The main house overlooking the paddocks has traditionally been the home of a Head Forester and there are two

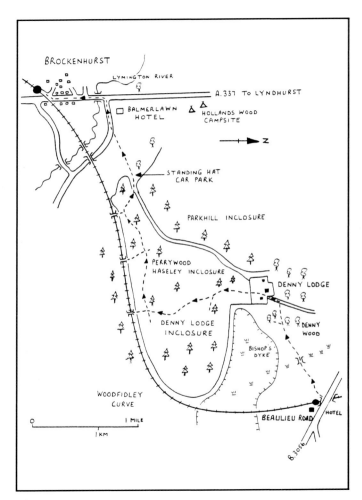

other cottages which once housed Forest workers. The small fields around the houses with cattle grazing, give the impression of a small self contained community but this is not true in today's Forest economy. As you pass down the hill the tarmac ends and your way is now on gravel tracks maintained by the Forestry Commission. Keep straight on the main track passing through a gate at the far end of the fields and into Denny Lodge Inclosure.

Standing Hat

Your route now continues southwards for about one mile and you should keep to what is obviously the main path ignoring all temptations to explore the many attractive looking rides that lead off into the Forest. Denny Lodge Inclosure contains a great

Denny Lodge on the walk to Brockenhurst. The main house is allocated to a Head Forester.   *Malcolm S. Trigg*

variety of tree types and ages and makes for an interesting walk although there are no views of course. This is made up for by the abundance of wildlife and there is a good chance of seeing deer if you are quiet. In about a mile you will come to a crossroads of gravel tracks with the edge of the inclosure and the railway just beyond. Turn right here to follow a gravel track that runs parallel to the railway. This is now Perrywood Haseley Inclosure although as in so many other cases the inclosures have been joined together without any fences between them. Keep to the gravel track which bends south at one point to be near the railway before passing through another named inclosure — Pignalhill. The path now leaves the inclosure by a gate and comes out into the open by a Forestry Commission car-park called Standing Hat. The word 'hat' derives from the word 'holm' (holly) and usually applies to small copses. From Standing Hat follow the gravel track towards Brockenhurst which is now just over one mile away.

Balmer Lawn

The track leads across a wide open plain dotted with trees and gorse bushes known as Balmer Lawn. In the trees on its western side is one of the largest campsites at Hollands Wood. The track joins the B3055 on the outskirts of Brockenhurst and you should turn right to follow this to its junction with the A35. By this junction is the large Balmer Lawn Hotel which was used by American troops in the build up to 'D'-Day in the second world war. As Supreme Allied Commander, Eisenhower visited his troops at the Balmer Lawn and he passed through the New Forest frequently in the months leading up to 'D'-Day. Nowadays the riverside lawn by the hotel is a favourite spot for holiday makers in the summer months. The river is the Lymington River and you cross this and follow the A35 into the village where you will soon see the level crossing and the entrance to the station on the right. There are numerous hotels, cafes and pubs in this area but the main village is to be found to the west of the main road.

BROCKENHURST TO
BANK (Near Lyndhurst)

The main part of this walk is along the banks of the Highland Water stream and it takes you through some of the most majestic areas of old woodlands in the centre of the New Forest. It is planned as a circular walk but you can easily extend it to Lyndhurst from where there is the option of returning to Brockenhurst by bus. A detour along the way also allows you to visit the New Forest reptiliary.

Brockenhurst has a station that is much larger than you would expect for a village of modest size. This is because it is the junction for the Lymington branch and in recent years it has been developed as a 'railhead' for much of the Forest. Good road access, a large car park and a frequent service which sees all trains on the line stop here, means it is a busy station. From the 'up' side exit walk along the approach road to the main road and turn left by the level crossing. Turn left again immediately past the Morant Arms and go along Brookley Road towards the village centre.

The Watersplash

Brookley Road will soon bring you to the village centre with its shops lining the mainly Victorian main street. You will find plenty of opportunity to stock up on supplies if you intend to have a picnic on the course of your walk. The main street is still accessible to the Forest animals and you are quite likely to encounter ponies or donkeys. Please remember however, not to feed them as it is against the Forest bye-laws, and you will soon find what a nuisance and danger they can be. At the far end of the main street is an attractive ford across a small Forest stream and this spot is well known as 'the watersplash'. Once over this turn right at a 'T'-junction and walk along Rhinefield Road.

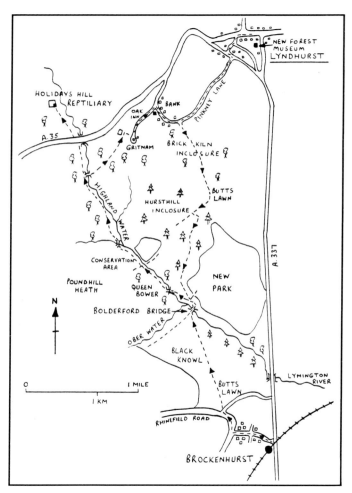

NEW FOREST
MUSEUM
LYNDHURST

HOLIDAYS HILL
REPTILIARY

A.35

BANK

OAK
INN

GRITNAM

PINKNEY LANE

BRICK KILN
INCLOSURE

BUTTS
LAWN

HIGHLAND WATER

HURSTHILL
INCLOSURE

A.337

CONSERVATION
AREA

POUNDHILL
HEATH

QUEEN
BOWER

NEW
PARK

N

BOLDERFORD BRIDGE

OBER WATER

BLACK
KNOWL

LYMINGTON
RIVER

0   1 MILE

1 KM

BUTTS
LAWN

RHINEFIELD ROAD

BROCKENHURST

62

Black Knoll

In about ¼ mile you will come to another 'T'-junction on the edge of open Forest land overlooked by large residential properties. At this point you will see a clear Forest track heading away from the road junction in a north-nor-easterly direction. This will take you across Butts Lawn, a grassy area with a small enclosed area on your right which surprisingly contains allotments. The path continues for about a mile across an undulating area of heathland known as Black Knoll. You will be heading for the diagonally opposite corner of this open area which is surrounded by woodland.

The Clapham Junction of Forest Paths

You will eventually come to a gravel track on the far side of Black Knoll and as you turn right onto it you will soon find yourself entering the woodland at Bolderford Bridge. This bridge crosses a large river which downstream is known as the Lymington River and upstream of this point is known as Highland Water. In fact several small streams join the main river here and this fact coupled with the fact that many paths radiate from this central point led a writer from an earlier age to christen this spot as 'the Clapham Junction' of Forest paths! In fact it is quite easy to find your way from Bolderford Bridge as the path you want generally follows the main river upstream.

Queen Bower

Once over the river at Bolderford Bridge keep to the path that swings away to your left heading north-east. Do not follow the main gravel track which enters an inclosure, although if you follow the circular walk via Bank you will return along this path. Your way now lies amongst some majestic old oak and beech trees and the path (which can be muddy) soon crosses the river by a bridge, with a seat conveniently placed alongside. This might prove to be a good spot for a quiet rest under the magnificent trees as there is a long walk ahead of you. Queen

Walking beneath the mighty oak trees in Queen Bower near Brockenhurst.
Malcolm S. Trigg

Bower is said to have been the favourite walk of Queen Eleanor, wife of Edward I.

Conservation Area

The path now takes a very pleasant and interesting route alongside the Highland Water stream as you follow it upstream. Your way is still through areas of old deciduous trees and indeed the rest of the outward part of this walk is through similar countryside. There are occasional views to the west across pockets of heathland such as Poundhill Heath. This is a very quiet and remote spot and is a haven for all manner of wildlife. It is not surprising therefore when you come across a Forestry Commission sign proclaiming this to be a 'conservation area'. You are asked not to cause any unnecessary disturbance, but to the keen walker who appreciates this wonderful environment, this is not asking anything out of the ordinary. The path soon comes to a cross-roads with a gravel track but you continue straight on following the stream. On your right, and on the far bank of the stream, is an enclosed field surrounded by trees which is a popular haunt for grazing deer. This secluded spot is overlooked by a Forestry Commission hide and viewing platform which is only open by special arrangement.

Brinken Wood

Just beyond the wildlife hide a tributary stream joins the river and a footbridge takes you over this. You will now find yourself in a broad Forest glade. The path takes a fairly well defined course through this avenue of trees with the river meandering some way to your right. In about ¼ mile the path rejoins the river and follows it closely again. There are several ox-bow lakes visible beside the river along this stretch, and these are the remains of old river meanders which have been isolated from the main channel by erosion. This area of ancient trees is Brinken Wood and it is a delightful place especially in summer when the Forest is alive with all manner of wildlife. The trees are home to a great variety of birds, and squirrels are

The New Forest Reptiliary at Holidays Hill.

Malcolm S. Trigg

everywhere. Ponies graze freely under the Forest giants and the river is a world of its own. Dragonflies and butterflies are attracted to the waterside and the river contains many small fish which can be seen darting over the gravel bed and under the mossy banks. Many wild flowers adorn these woods in summer and the autumn scene can be quite magnificent. You may well want to linger in this attractive area but if you keep going you will come to a small bridge over the river. This is within sound of traffic on the A35 main road to Bournemouth and you will have walked 3½ miles to reach this spot. Your way lies over the bridge but a short detour will be mentioned at this point in case you are interested.

Detour to the Reptiliary

The Forestry Commission maintains a reptiliary at Holidays Hill near here. If you want to see this do not cross the bridge but continue on the path for about ⅓ mile until you reach the A35. Cross this busy road and on the opposite side is a gravel track leading to Holidays Hill. This area was laid out for an informal campsite, but at the time of writing it has been taken out of use because there is excess capacity following a downturn in camping numbers. The gravel track follows the course of Highland Water for about ½ mile until you come to a Keepers cottage and the entrance to the reptiliary. This consists of several large concrete 'tanks' which contain examples of all the reptiles found in the New Forest including adders, grass snakes, the rare smooth snake and the endangered sand lizard. The reptiliary is used for educational purposes as well as providing a breeding area from which rare species can be released into the wild to maintain the numbers. There is no entrance charge but a leaflet is available for a small charge and there are also toilets on the site which is open from March — October from 8.00 a.m. to 8.00 p.m. This detour makes for a very interesting visit and you should now retrace your steps, crossing the main road and finding the bridge in Brinken Wood.

Gritnam and Bank

Cross the bridge and follow a clear path through the trees which gradually climbs uphill away from the river in a north-easterly direction. Keep along this path for about ½ mile until it levels out and then keep a look out for a small fenced area on your left which contains some pumping equipment belonging to the water company. A gravel road leads from this to the A35 but your route does not lie in that direction. As you pass the water-works turn sharp right through the trees and very soon you should come across the small community of Gritnam. This consists of a few Forest cottages at the end of a narrow tarmac road. Follow this road for ½ mile until you come to the more substantial community of Bank. You are definitely back in civilisation now and you can find welcome refreshment at the Oak Inn (formerly the Royal Oak). Bank is a residential area of Forest cottages and more substantial (and very expensive) country houses. It is really an outer part of Lyndhurst but forms a distinct community and the main village is still about 1 mile away.

Pinkney Lane

From the Oak Inn turn right along the road which passes through the houses (i.e. away from the main road) which takes you to the south of Lyndhurst whose church spire should be visible. The lane then turns sharp left and passes over a cattle grid. This is Pinkney Lane and if you want to visit Lyndhurst this quiet road will take you there in about 1 mile. For details of Lyndhurst, the 'capital' of the New Forest see walk No. 3 but you should note that it is possible to return to Brockenhurst by the hourly bus service. If you do not wish to spend time in Lyndhurst do not go down Pinkney Lane, but once over the cattle-grid referred to above, turn right into Brick Kiln Inclosure and follow a gravel track.

New Park

It is now a fairly straightforward route back to Bolderford Bridge along gravel tracks through various inclosures. Brick Kiln Inclosures has in fact now been 'thrown open' i.e. the fences removed so that animals can freely graze. This is often done when the trees are of substantial age and there is no danger of grazing causing too much damage. The path continues steadily downhill and crosses an open area of heath called Butts Lawn, which was once outside the inclosure. The track turns right and soon comes to a junction where you should turn sharp left to enter New Park Plantation. As you continue along the gravel track you will notice through the trees some open fields to your left which is New Park. This dates from 1291 and was added to by Charles II in 1670 for the preservation of red deer, newly introduced from France. It is an extensive area of parkland now used as the venue for the annual New Forest Show in July and the main entrance is on the Lyndhurst to Brockenhurst road. At this time the Forest tracks are used as part of a one-way traffic flow from Lyndhurst to get visiting vehicles off the main roads and into the show-site. This walk would thus best not be done on those three days at the end of July as the usual peace and quiet will be spoilt! After walking about 2 miles from Pinkney Lane you will come to another junction where you turn right, and passing through an inclosure gate come to Bolderford Bridge which you passed on the outward part of the walk. It is now straightforward to retrace your steps to Brockenhurst village, for some more refreshment, and thence to the station.

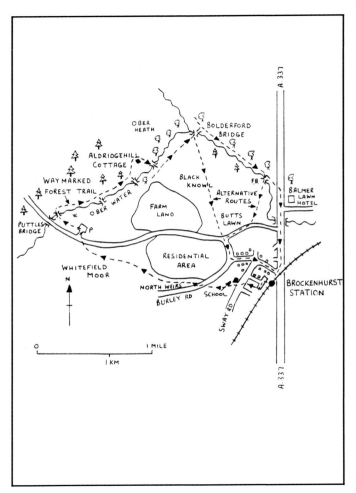

OBER HEATH

BOLDERFORD BRIDGE

ALDRIDGEHILL COTTAGE

WAY MARKED FOREST TRAIL

BLACK KNOWL

OBER WATER

ALTERNATIVE ROUTES

F.B.

BALMER LAWN HOTEL

PUTTLES BRIDGE

FARM LAND

P

BUTTS LAWN

A 337

WHITEFIELD MOOR

RESIDENTIAL AREA

BROCKENHURST STATION

NORTH WEIRS

BURLEY RD

SCHOOL

SWAY RD

N

0   1 MILE

1 KM

70

BROCKENHURST TO OBER WATER

This circular walks takes you from Brockenhurst station to one of the Forestry Commission's specially laid out waymarked trails. After following most of the trail your way continues along the course of the Ober Water until it joins Highland Water and becomes the Lymington river. Most of the walk is along easy paths which are usually quite dry and there is an interesting variety of Forest habitats to enjoy.

Leave Brockenhurst station by the booking office on the 'up' side and instead of following the main exit route, cross the car park and look for a pedestrian exit on to East Bank Road. Turn left and at the end of the road turn right over a stile and follow a footpath which brings you to Sway Road opposite the village school. This route misses the village centre but the walk is planned to bring you back that way on the return when you may welcome the refreshment facilities offered there.

North Weirs

Cross the Sway Road by the school and you will find a gravel path leading north-west which will take you across fields to the Burley road and you should turn left onto this for a short way. This road is bordered by a broad grassy area on either side with large residences on the north side set well back from the road. As you follow the road look out for a gravel road to your right signposted 'North Weirs'. This track, which serves the houses on this western part of the village, gradually takes you away from the road. After about ½ mile the track turns right and a broad grassy plain opens out in front of you. This is Whitefield Moor and is a war-time re-seeded area which is now popular with grazing cattle and ponies. There is no particular path to follow here but head out across the plain in a north-westerly direction and you will see ahead of you a minor road. Follow the general direction of this road until you see a large car park surrounded by gorse bushes on the edge of a valley with trees beyond. This is Whitefield Moor car park and the start of the Forest trail known as Ober Water Walk.

Ober Water

It is just as well to buy a leaflet from the dispenser at the start of the Forest Walk as this has a map and gives a lot of useful background information. There are also information posts at frequent intervals along the walk to give added interest to what you can see. The path descends from the car park across heathland down to the tree lined river which you cross by a wooden bridge. The Ober Water is an attractive meandering stream and the path follows its course along its northern bank with Aldridgehill inclosure to your left. This is an old inclosure containing some attractive oak woodlands and it has now been thrown open (i.e. the fences removed). You should follow the marker posts indicated for the longer of the two waymarked trails and this will eventually bring you to the second bridge.

Aldridgehill Cottage

The waymarked trail crosses the river at this point but unless you are particularly anxious to complete the trail (which ends up back at Whitefield Moor car park necessitating quite a detour) you should not cross the bridge but turn left onto a path leading away from the stream and up into the woods. This path will soon bring you to an attractive Keepers cottage on the edge of Ober Heath. This expansive Heath is a deserted place for much of the year but in the summer there is an informal but popular campsite along the southern edge adjoining the river. Follow the main track from the cottage to cross the river and then turn left onto a narrow tarmac road.

Bolderford Bridge

The tarmac road soon ends and beyond a car-free zone barrier it becomes a gravel track. In about ½ mile you will reach

Bolderford Bridge where the river joins Highland Water flowing from the north and the combined waters flow south as the Lymington River. You can continue to follow the river by crossing the bridge and walking along the east bank. This section of about one mile is again through deciduous woodland and will bring you out onto the A35 opposite the Balmer Lawn Hotel where you should turn right and follow the main road to the station. Before the main road is reached a footbridge over the river gives access to the southern edge of Butts Lawn and the village centre is easily reached via Meerut Road as an alternative route. Another quicker route from Bolderford Bridge is to head directly south-south-west across Black Knoll and Butts lawn back to the village centre and thence back to the station. (see map).

The King Rufus pub at Eling, near Totton. Although not inside the New Forest perambulation, this area has strong historical links with the Forest.   *Malcolm S. Trigg*

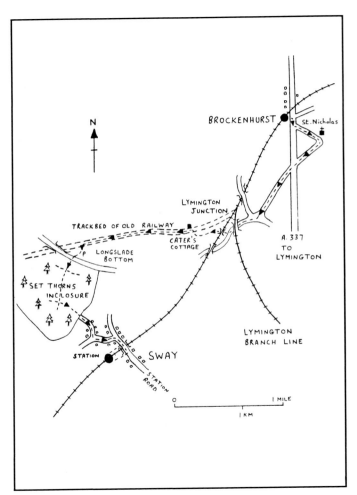

N

BROCKENHURST St. Nicholas

LYMINGTON
JUNCTION

TRACKBED OF OLD RAILWAY

CATER'S
COTTAGE

A.337
TO
LYMINGTON

LONGSLADE
BOTTOM

SET THORNS
INCLOSURE

LYMINGTON
BRANCH LINE

STATION SWAY

STATION
ROAD

0   1 MILE

1 KM

BROCKENHURST TO SWAY

This inter-station walk is partly along the old trackbed of the original railway route across the New Forest from Brockenhurst to Holmsley and on towards Ringwood. After closure the trackbed reverted to Forestry Commission ownership and now provides a firm level footpath. This walk could be combined with part of walk 16 to complete the journey along the trackbed to the old Holmsley station tearooms.

The Forest's Oldest Church

Leave Brockenhurst station by the 'down' side exit and cross the car park to the main road. This first part of the walk will avoid walking along main roads and will provide some interest in Forest matters even if it does not seem to be the most direct route. Turn right and, ignoring Mill Lane which is directly opposite, look for the next turning on the left which is a small lane leading uphill away from the main road. This lane leads to St. Nicholas' church which is at the top of the hill and from which there are views over the village. St. Nicholas' church is the oldest in the New Forest and has occupied this site since 800 A.D. The Norman builders in 1086 used some of the Saxon walling for the building and the church is well worth visiting.

Brusher Mills

There is an extensive graveyard and amongst the tombstones is a distinctive one inscribed to Henry "Brusher" Mills who died in 1905. A lot has been written about this eccentric character who lived in a hut in the Forest and made a living as a snake catcher, selling adders to various institutions including London Zoo. Incidentally, the old Railway Inn near Brockenhurst station is now called 'The Snake Catcher'. The origin of his nickname 'Brusher' is a matter for debate but some say it was because he brushed the cricket pitch at Lyndhurst

St. Nicholas Church at Brockenhurst — the oldest in the New Forest. *Malcolm S. Trigg*

to keep it playable. After this diversion to see the church and graveyard continue along the lane which now turns south-west. To your left is the parkland of Brockenhurst Park and the lane actually follows the Forest boundary. In about ½ mile you will come to the main road (A337) which you should cross to continue along another quiet lane.

Lymington Junction

Continue along this lane for about ½ mile until you come to a 'T'-junction where you turn right. This road soon dips sharply to pass underneath the Lymington branch line. At this point the single track line is swinging south from the main line which it originally left at Lymington Junction just to your right. Nowadays the line runs independently from, and parallel to, the main line all the way from Brockenhurst station. As you pass under the bridge you will seen the main line to Bournemouth ahead of you on an embankment. As the road swings round to the left look for a gravel track leading off to the right and passing under the railway and through a brick underbridge. This track leads across heathland and in about ½ mile you will come to the trackbed of the original railway line.

Cater's Cottage

As you approach the old railway you will see the unmistakable outline of an old gate-keepers cottage, now painted white. This once guarded a level crossing giving access to Cater's cottage. Only the gate posts now remain but the trackbed is clear and you should turn left to follow the old railway. The first part is a deep tree-lined cutting through Blackhamsley Hill and this rather dank place can be very damp under foot at times. However, you will soon come out into the open and the way is now along a low embankment giving easy walking conditions and pleasant views. You will continue along the old railway for about one mile and there is an overbridge that has unfortunately been removed necessitating a minor detour at one point.

Old railway crossing Keeper's cottage at Cater's Cottage. This is on the old line to Ringwood which closed in 1964.

Malcolm S. Trigg

Setthorns Inclosure

When the trackbed comes to a second dismantled bridge you should come down from the embankment and turn left to reach a car park known as Longslade Bottom. (If you want to make the longer walk combined with walk 16, keep straight on here). From the car park cross the road to enter Setthorns inclosure and follow the gravel track straight ahead of you. This leads into a mature coniferous plantation and you should follow the gravel track for about   mile, keeping straight on at the first cross-roads, until you come to a second cross-roads in the heart of the inclosure. Turn left here and another gravel track will take you gradually down hill to the south-eastern edge of the inclosure.

Sway

As you leave the inclosure you will cross a broad grass drove (open land left to allow animals access between enclosed areas such as this) and there is another gate opposite leading to a gravel track going uphill. This track crosses farmland and at the top of the hill meets a small tarmac road called Adlam's Lane. This lane serves a residential area on the edge of Sway village and at the end you should turn left into Mead End Lane. In a short distance this road meets Station Road and you turn right to reach the station at Sway. The village shops are strung out along this road and you will find plenty of opportunities for places of refreshment at the end of this walk.

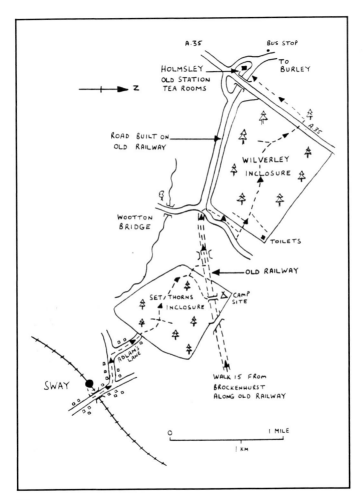

N

BUS STOP

A.35

TO BURLEY

HOLMSLEY OLD STATION TEA ROOMS

A.35

ROAD BUILT ON OLD RAILWAY

WILVERLEY INCLOSURE

WOOTTON BRIDGE

TOILETS

OLD RAILWAY

SET THORNS INCLOSURE

CAMP SITE

ADLAM'S LANE

SWAY

WALK 15 FROM BROCKENHURST ALONG OLD RAILWAY

0   1 MILE

1 KM

SWAY TO HOLMSLEY

This walk starts in the village of Sway which is on the edge of the New Forest. The walk takes you through two attractive inclosures and also along part of the old railway to Holmsley where the station is now an attractive tearoom. A bus service from here can be used to take a scenic ride back to the railway at Lyndhurst Road station. (Ashurst).

From Sway station turn left at the top of the entrance road into Station Road which has a number of useful shops and pubs etc. In about ½ mile turn left into Mead End Road and then look for the next turning on your right marked Adlam's Lane — a 'no through road'. This residential lane soon ends and the way becomes a gravel track descending into a valley through farm land. Ahead of you is Setthorns Inclosure and you should continue through two gates to enter the Forest.

Setthorns

Your path is now a gravel track through an inclosure of mature coniferous trees and you should continue uphill until a crossroads of paths is reached. Keep straight on and the path gradually turns to your right. In about one mile after entering the inclosure the path descends and turns more sharply to the right to enter the site of Setthorns campsite. Before you reach the campsite look out for a gate to your left which leads out of the inclosure and onto heathland. Once through the gate follow a well defined path heading north-east and ahead of you is the unmistakable embankment of the old railway line with a brick arch of an underbridge.

The Old Railway

It should be fairly easy to scramble up onto the top of the embankment and you will then find a good flat path along the old trackbed. You should continue to walk along the old railway

The old railway trackbed crosses Setthorns campsite near Sway. *Malcolm S. Trigg*

until you come to the point where it is taken over by a new road which stretches away in a straight line ahead of you towards Holmsley. You are advised not to continue walking along this road as it is quite busy and there is no pavement so an alternative route is given through Wilverley inclosure.

Peterson's Folly

When you leave the trackbed turn right and carefully cross the new road and on slightly higher ground you will find the remains of an old road which provides safe walking. Continue along this path with Wilverley Lodge to your left and the road to Brockenhurst to your right. As you look back to the south there is a good view over Sway and away to the Isle of Wight in the distance. A clear landmark to look out for is a tall tower known variously as Sway Tower, Peterson's Tower or Peterson's Folly. This tower which is 218 feet tall was built in 1884 and was one man's attempt to prove the value of concrete as a building material. It has stood the test of time and nowadays the lower floors have been converted into an unusual hotel.

Wilverley

Your way now runs parallel to the fence of Wilverley inclosure and you should look for a Forestry Commission car park on your left. From this car park there is a waymarked trail through Wilverley inclosure and you will be following part of this to avoid the aforementioned road along the old railway and to end up at Holmsley station tea-rooms. Follow the main gravel track into the inclosure and keep to this path for about 1¼ miles until you reach the A35 main road.

Holmsley

Cross the main road and turn left to follow it south-westwards. The land soon dips down and the line of the old railway will be visible in the valley below. A path leads downhill and you cross a stile to reach the old station. The main station buildings remain and have been converted into an attractive complex of

tea-rooms providing an attractive setting for refreshments at the end of your walk. If you want to return by bus, the bus stop is just around the corner on the road towards Burley. A two-hourly (not Sundays) limited bus service from Southampton to Ringwood passes this spot (Wilts & Dorset service X1) and the easiest way to get back to a railway station in the New Forest is to take a Southampton bound bus to Ashurst, for Lyndhurst Road station. The limited stop bus service only stops at one point in Ashurst village and you will have to walk for about half a mile back to the station.

Left: Holmsley station is now a popular tea room. The cars are on the old trackbed of the line from Brockenhurst to Ringwood.

Malcolm S. Trigg

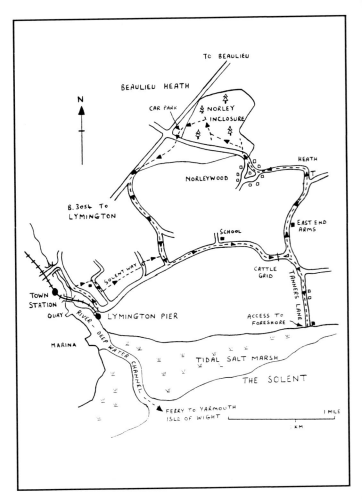

TO BEAULIEU

BEAULIEU HEATH

N

CAR PARK

NORLEY INCLOSURE

HEATH

NORLEYWOOD

B.3054 TO LYMINGTON

EAST END ARMS

SCHOOL

CATTLE GRID

TANNERS LANE

TOWN STATION

QUAY

LYMINGTON PIER

SOLENT WAY

ACCESS TO FORESHORE

MARINA

RIVER — DEEP WATER CHANNEL

TIDAL SALT MARSH

THE SOLENT

FERRY TO YARMOUTH ISLE OF WIGHT

1 MILE

KM

WALK SEVENTEEN: Approximately 9 miles (14.5 km)

LYMINGTON PIER TO NORLEYWOOD

This circular walk takes you to the southern edge of the New Forest where the perambulation comes down to the shores of the Solent. It commences along a footpath which is part of the Solent Way long distance waymarked path but much of the remainder has to be along country roads. For this reason this walk may best be done in the off-season when the other Forest walks may be too wet and the roads in this case will be at their quietest.

Lymington Pier

The Lymington branch provides a delightful short journey across the southern part of the New Forest and is a reminder of what a country branch line was like. The first station is Lymington Town where the platform signs remind you that you should stay on the train for the next station for the Isle of Wight ferries. The branch line then crosses the Lymington River by a viaduct from which there is a good view of the old town and the river which is nowadays crammed with yachts. The train draws to a halt alongside a wooden pier and the ferry will be seen waiting at its berth at the end of a walkway from the end of the platform. Avoid the temptation to board the ferry for the Isle of Wight if you want to do this walk, but there is the compensation that the Island will be in view for much of your way!

The Solent Way

From the exit at Lymington Pier station cross the large car park to the road and turn left back towards Lymington. In about 250 yards the road joins the river wall and at this point you should turn right up a gravel path and look for a stile with the Solent Way signpost (a seagull symbol). A footpath takes you steeply

87

Tanners Lane where the New Forest meets the Solent. Beyond the saltmarsh the Isle of Wight is visible.

Malcolm S. Trigg

uphill towards a tall monument that is a landmark for some distance around. The monument is to Sir Harry Burrard Neale who was the local M.P. as well as a famous Admiral before his death in 1840. There ought to be some fine views from the monument on top of the hill but unfortunately they are mostly obscured by dense trees. Turn right onto a narrow road and follow this for about 200 yards until you see a gravel path to your left. This looks like a private drive to a bungalow but there is a right of way as part of the Solent Way and you will soon find a field gate leading to the actual footpath. The path now follows a pleasant route along the top of a ridge, crossing farmland and with pleasant views southwards over the Solent to the Isle of Wight. You should follow the path for about mile until you come to a small road. At this point turn left and then very soon right along a gravel path through Snooks Farm. This is all part of the Solent Way and you should have no trouble finding the special symbols to guide you. In about 300 yards the gravel track meets another country lane and your way is now along quiet roads but still part of the Solent Way. Turn right and then left at the crossroads to join the road towards South Baddesley and East End.

Tanners Lane

Follow the road for about 1½ miles, past the isolated junior school at South Baddesley, until you cross a cattle grid and come to a T-junction. The grid marks the official boundary of the New Forest and from now on there is the possibility of encountering animals wandering along these quiet lanes. At the T-junction your way ultimately leads to the left but it is strongly recommended that you take a detour here to walk down Tanners Lane to one of the rare point where there is public access to the shore within the Forest perambulation. Turn right and at the next junction keep straight on where the road to Sowley turns sharp left. This is Tanners Lane and it is difficult to imagine a more tranquil spot as the lane leads gently down to the Solent shore. There are a few cottages and then the lane

Norley Wood – a typical New Forest car park and picnic site. The Scots Pine provide an attractive setting.

Malcolm S. Trigg

suddenly ends at the water's edge. No car park or cafe or any other seaside 'attraction' — just the Solent lapping gently at a stoney shore with saltmarsh stretching away in all directions. This is a haven for bird life and many migrating species can be seen at the appropriate time of year in this area which is a nature reserve. Most of the New Forest foreshore is now inaccessible because of private ownership but this delightful spot is a reminder of what it was like in days gone by. You will now need to retrace your steps to the junction by the cattle grid and head northwards.

Eastenders

The road heads north and then north-east towards the scattered village of East End. Before this is reached you will pass the East End Arms pub on the right hand side of the road. The people living here must surely have a vastly different lifestyle to the other Eastenders of T.V. fame! The houses of East End are reached in about one mile and you should turn left by a telephone box onto a road signed to Norleywood. The road now skirts the edge of the open Forest and you can walk on the heath for a short distance if you are tired of road walking. Incidentally, this part of the walk is on a bus route (Wilts & Dorset service 112 from Lymington to Hythe) and so you have an alternative way back should you need it.

Norleywood

Keep to the road which leaves East End and meanders for about one mile through the scattered community of Norleywood. As is often the case in the countryside nowadays all local facilities such as shops seem to have closed down and the villages are mostly residential hideaways for those who commute to neighbouring towns. Nevertheless, Norleywood retains something of a rustic atmosphere and in what was once the village centre is a wooden bus shelter. Soon after this look out for Norleywood Cottage on the right hand side of the road beyond which is Norley inclosure. It is worth taking a route through the inclosure to avoid too much road walking and to enjoy a different environment to what has gone on before. (N.B. If conditions underfoot are too wet in the inclosure, continue along the road and rejoin the walk at the north-west corner of the inclosure). At the first gate on the right of the road enter the inclosure and follow a gravel track. Take the first grassy path on the left and follow this for about ¼ mile before turning right on to another grass track. In another ¼ mile turn left and this path will bring you out at Norleywood picnic site and car park. Walk through the car park following the inclosure fence until you rejoin the road. Cross the road, with a crossroads to your right, and follow a track across heathland which leads to the road (B3054) back to Lymington.

The Solent Way Regained

The road is rather busy, so turn left at the first opportunity and follow a quiet lane with the grounds of Newtown Park on your left. At a Y-junction keep right and as the lane gently descends so views of the Isle of Wight reappear in the distance. In about one mile you will come to the point where the Solent Way footpath joined the road earlier on in the walk. It should now be easy to retrace your steps, or if you prefer, you can take the road that runs parallel to the path to bring you back to Lymington Pier station and your train home.

A BRIEF HISTORY

The railway which now passes through the New Forest is part of the main line from London Waterloo to Weymouth and is electrified on the third rail system. It is heavily used by commuters, business travellers and by leisure travellers as it connects such important centres as Bournemouth, Poole, Southampton and Winchester to the capital. Such importance could not have been foreseen by the original promoters and indeed the original line did not comment all the places mentioned above.

Castleman's Corkscrew

The London to Southampton line was finished in 1840 and helped to establish the port whilst the area to the west remained mainly rural in character. Soon there was interest in building a line to the west of Southampton and Charles Castleman, a Wimborne solicitor, put forward a scheme in 1844 to build a line to Dorchester. The route finally selected took a very winding course and became known as ''Castleman's Corkscrew''. The circuitous route was partly the result of trying to link together the settlements of some importance and also because of difficulties in choosing a suitable course through the New Forest. The problems here concerned the need to avoid interference with the royal deer and also to avoid fires which might destroy the plantations of timber which at that time were still supplying much of the Royal Navy's needs.

Brunel's Compromise

From Southampton the line crossed the river Test between Redbridge and Totton and then turned south towards Lymington. At one time a coastal route through Beaulieu to Lymington and on towards Poole was proposed (Bournemouth did not exist at that time) but this was later abandoned to take in the established towns of Ringwood and Wimborne before heading west to Dorchester. Several routes through the Forest were examined and at one stage the famous engineer Brunel was called in to arbitrate and a compromise was finally reached. It was decided to avoid as much as possible of the main area of woodland which, then as now, occupies the centre of the New Forest. This decision, together with the fact that the residents of Lyndhurst were not keen to have the railway on their doorsteps, led to the line taking a large sweep to the south where it enters the Forest and to the building of Lyndhurst Road station some 2½ miles from the village. Beaulieu Road was another compromise location being some 4 miles from Beaulieu. For this reason it was never very successful and indeed it was closed between 1860 and 1895. Brockenhurst was thus the nearest station to Lymington, and later on it was destined to become an important station with lines diverging in three directions at Lymington Junction just to the west.

Horses Lost in the Construction

After Brockenhurst the line headed north-west towards Ringwood with a station being built at Holmsley (originally called Christchurch Road) where a horse bus gave connection to the important port of Christchurch. This stretch of line caused considerable troubles to the builders and following a winter of heavy rain the engineer lost no fewer than 11 horses in a few weeks during the course of cutting through a dangerous layer of clay. There are no major engineering works on the line which climbs to a summit near Beaulieu road and then follows a gently undulating course. The line which was at first single track, was opened in 1847 with the first test train operating from Lyndhurst to Dorchester on 1st May and public services starting on 1st June.

The Growth of Bournemouth

A single track branch line from Brockenhurst to Lymington was opened in 1858 and this was extended to Lymington Pier in 1884. In 1860 a halt was opened on the branch line at Shirley Holmes to serve the village of Sway to the west, as traffic grew on the main line so it was doubled during the period 1857−63. At that time Bournemouth was a tiny insignificant village and Poole was a traffic centre reached by a branch from Hamworthy Junction. However, as time went on so Bournemouth gradually developed as a fashionable resort and in time there was a demand for a railway connection. A branch from Ringwood to Christchurch was opened in 1862 and extended to Bournemouth in 1870. This route however, was very circuitous and in time was unable to cope with the growth of Bournemouth, so in 1888 a new line was built from Brockenhurst through Sway (Shirley Holmes was closed) to Christchurch, to give direct access to the new coastal resort. This soon became the main line (although until recent years tickets still had the routing 'via Sway' on them) and an important part of the London and South Western Railway system. From that time the original line via Ringwood gradually became a secondary route with a mainly local service although at busy holiday weekends it was used by trains to Weymouth and Swanage so by-passing the traffic bottleneck of Bournemouth. The line gradually lost business and it was closed in the Beeching cuts in 1964. The present line is thus a combination of part of the original 'Castleman's Corkscrew' and the later line of 1888 to Bournemouth.

Visitors by Rail

The railway was certainly one of the factors in developing the New Forest as a tourist attraction as it gave easy access in an area of poor roads. A contemporary account of 1893 tells of a special train from Millbrook (near Southampton) bringing 530 children and 150 adults to Lyndhurst Road for an annual 'Sunday School Treat', and one assumes this was a fairly unusual occurence. The Crown Hotel in Lyndhurst operated a horse-drawn carriage service to and from Lyndhurst Road around the turn of the century and the L.S.W.R. operated an early motor bus on the same route in 1904. In 1902 a plan was published for an electric light railway to be built linking Lyndhurst with its station but nothing came of this. In 1914 there were 14 trains in each direction serving Lyndhurst Road and the pattern of services was clearly arranged for passengers coming to the 'capital' of the forest rather than for the convenience of local people.

Modernisation

The line achieved some fame in the 1960s as it was the last main line to be worked by steam traction and the sight of Bullied Pacifics rushing across the New Forest heathlands is something fondly remembered by many people. The Lymington branch had a claim to fame as the last steam-worked branch line in Britain, but all this was too end in July 1967. At that time the line to Bournemouth and the Lymington branch were both electrified and so entered a new phase of their history. The stock used was the 4-REP traction units working on the push-pull principle with non powered TC trailer units and in this respect the line through the New Forest broke new ground in railway technology. In 1988 the line from Bournemouth to Weymouth was electrified and a new series of specially built trains introduced — the Class 442 'Wessex Electrics' which have brought the best ever service to the line. With ever increasing road congestion in the Forest it is to be hoped that the railway can once again become a significant mover of visitors, and that it will be seen as an environmentally friendly asset as the quiet electric trains sweep across the heathlands and through the woodlands.

SPECIAL NOTE: At the time of going to press (July 1993), 'Rambles by Rail 3 (The Matlock Line) had still not been published. This is regretted, but is due to none delivery of the copy by the author.

The JUICE 2010

by
Matt Skinner

The Juice 2010
by Matt Skinner

The Juice Team
and Mitchell Beazley
would like to send
a big thank you to
all the wine merchants,
agents, retailers, and
producers who helped
with the research for
this edition of the book.

Disclaimer: Wherever possible the
current release of each wine has
been selected in line with the vintage
availability supplied by the winery
and/or agent or importer. Vintage and
recommended retail price information
is correct as far as possible, but
demand can affect which vintage is
available, and continuing taxation
of alcohol throughout the year by the
government affects price, upwards!

In wine entries the names of the
main retailers in the UK are shown,
but in many cases there will be others.
Please contact the winery or agent
or importer shown at the bottom of
the wine's retailer list and in the A–Z
stockist list at the back of the book
for the most up-to-date information
on your chosen wine(s) and your
nearest retailer.

First published in Great Britain in 2009
by Mitchell Beazley, an imprint of
Octopus Publishing Group Ltd,
2–4 Heron Quays, London E14 4JP.
www.octopusbooks.co.uk

An Hachette UK Company
www.hachettelivre.co.uk

ISBN 978 1 84533 518 2

A CIP catalogue record for this book is
available from the British Library.

Set in Helvetica Neue LT and AG Book Stencil
Colour reproduction by United Graphics, Singapore
Printed and bound by Toppan, China

The author and publishers will be grateful for any
information that will assist them in keeping future
editions up to date. Although all reasonable care
has been taken in the preparation of this book,
neither the publishers nor the author can accept
any liability for any consequences arising from the
use thereof, or the information contained therein.

Commissioning Editor Rebecca Spry
Editorial Director Tracey Smith
Managing Editor Hilary Lumsden
Senior Editor Leanne Bryan
Copy-editor Susanna Forbes
Proofreader Jo Richardson
Art Director Pene Parker
Concept Design Matt Utber
Layout Design Spencer Lawrence
Photographer Chris Terry
Production Manager Peter Hunt

Contents

It's a jungle out there

That's for sure. Unemployment is up. Spending is down. Times are tough. Better news is that as non-essential purchases swiftly become a thing of the past, history would suggest that a regular bottle of wine won't be one of them. From fancy holidays to new undies, it seems that there's plenty of things we're prepared to go without, but thankfully wine doesn't seem to be one of them.

Welcome to the value edition of *The Juice*. And while digging up bargains has always been close to my heart, this year I've made an extra-special effort to shine the spotlight on the wines that will ultimately give you more for less. And then I got to thinking, rather than simply saving you money, how else can wine add value to your life? Beyond the obvious, I came up with a few suggestions that, fingers crossed, should help you endure the gloomy times that are upon us.

For starters, dine consciously. How long has it been since you last shared a bottle of wine and a decent conversation over a home-cooked meal? Shop locally. Independent wine stores around the globe need you now more than ever – get to know those in your local area, take their advice, buy their wines, and help keep them trading. Bring your own. Find out which restaurants in your area have a BYO licence and support them. Buy a wine book. You'll watch less TV as a result, and you might even learn something along the way! Open your mind. Often the best- value wines are those from lesser-known varieties and places. Start a wine group. Not the kind where you sit around flexing your knowledge – the kind where everyone brings a bottle, you taste, you talk, you listen, and you laugh. Visit a vineyard. Just like your local wine shop, local producers need your support. If you live within striking range of a wine region, make a day of it – or better still, stay for the weekend!

Keep smiling x

How it all works

What began life as a weekly email sent out to friends and workmates in a vain attempt to help them drink better has now become a regular distillation of my drinking year. As with previous years, *The Juice 2010* combines 100 wine recommendations together with a few handy tips and a little bit of wisdom. Think of it as the big kids' survival guide to Planet Wine, or better still, a huge step toward better drinking.

So here's the drill. I thought that rather than ranking the wines 1 to 100, it'd be far more useful if I grouped the wines by occasion, and so this year I've split my 100 wines into four easy groups of 25 wines each: Skint, Dine, Drink, and Splurge. Bearing in mind the tough times we're all in the middle of, I have been on the lookout even more for wines that over-deliver on value. As always, there's something here for everyone: every taste, every budget, and every occasion.

As per last year, I've made every effort to ensure that both price and vintage are as accurate as possible at the time of publication (*see also* page 2). Listed stockists are a mixture of supermarkets, national chains, smaller independent wine retailers, and online merchants – the idea being that you should be able to get your hands on most of the following 100 wines without too much heartache.

Happy drinking!

Awards time always brings about a certain sense of dread. For starters, there is very deliberately no ranking system in *The Juice*, there are no star ratings, and no scores out of 100. Pedestals are not what this guide has ever been about. Irrespective of price, each of the wines featured in this book deserves to be here for one reason or another. That said, throughout the course of the year there are always one or two wines – and one or two names – that repeatedly crop up, and for that reason I think it's important you know what and who they are. So without apology, these are the wines that I talked about, enthused about, and repeatedly sniffed, swirled, and slurped this year.

Wine of the year

Castellare di Castellina Chianti Classico 2007
Tuscany, Italy

For many years Castellare have made, and continue to make, beautiful wine – simple as that. Located high up (370 metres, 1200 feet) in the postcard-like hills of Castellina in Chianti, this estate, owned by Paolo Panerai since 1979, bucks the trend for power and concentration, producing traditionally styled wines from its 33 hectares with breathtaking purity and great elegance.

From the warmth of the 2007 vintage, this is an incredibly pure snapshot of Sangiovese, where a nose of pure morello cherry, leather, and tobacco make way for a plush, mineral-textured palate framed by trademark chalky Sangiovese tannins, fresh acidity, and a clean, drying finish. With hunting prohibited on the estate, Castellare also doubles as a natural wildlife refuge for many local animals – including the (annually changing) wild birds that feature on the front labels. A simply outstanding wine from an outstanding producer. (*See* page 179.)

THE JUICE AWARDS 2010

Bargain of the year

d'Arenberg
The Stump Jump 2007
McLaren Vale, Australia

Since 1943, d'Arry Osborne has firmly focused his attention on handcrafting some of the most high-quality examples of Grenache and Syrah produced anywhere in the New World. Armed with a traditional basket press, plenty of enthusiasm, and some of the oldest plantings (c.1890) of these varieties to be found outside of France's southern Rhône Valley, this estate is now regarded as one of the finest of its kind. That said, one of the most endearing qualities of d'Arenberg is that as consistently good as the wines are – and that's very good – they continue to remain consistently affordable.

The Stump Jump red, an all-terrain blend of unwooded bush vine Grenache (50 per cent), Shiraz (29 per cent), and Mourvèdre (21 per cent), is a great example of exactly that. Like other wines in the d'Arenberg range, production includes fermentation in head-down, open-top fermenters followed by gentle basket-pressing. (See page 106.)

Producer of the year

Dr Loosen
Germany

With holdings throughout Germany's most famed vineyards together with ecologically sound and sustainable practices, Ernie Loosen is widely regarded as not only one of the finest exponents of Riesling anywhere but as one of the greatest white winemakers on the planet.

His most basic offering, Dr L Riesling, is an accessible and pretty wine that walks the tightrope between sweetness and acidity with ease, while his most sought-after wines from the super-steep, south-facing, free-draining, slate-ridden vineyards between Bernkastel and Kindel are the stuff of legend. And although there have been numerous joint ventures around the world, Loosen has always been a fierce champion of the German wine industry, of the integrity of its wines, of valuing quality over quantity, and for bending over backwards to reintroduce quality German wine to the rest of the world. (See page 126.)

Varieties, places, & styles

Wine comes in all different shapes and sizes; big wines, little wines, fat wines, skinny wines, good wines, great wines, and wines that will absolutely blow your mind. And while what happens in the winery can play a big role in determining how a wine might end up tasting, grape variety, place, and style will all have an impact too. With the number of varieties and styles now running well into four figures, here's a brief rundown of those that grace the pages of this year's edition of *The Juice*.

The Whites

Chablis
(sha-blee)

Chablis is the name of a town in the northern-most part of Burgundy in France. The area's ancient Kimmeridgian limestone soils are unique and produce fine, pristine, mineral-like white wines, made out of Burgundy's white star, Chardonnay. With the use of new oak largely frowned upon in Chablis, the best examples display soft stone/citrus fruit, honey, river-rock, hay, mineral, and cashew character. And trademark mouth-watering acidity ensures that these wines are with us for years.

Chardonnay
(SHAR-do-nay)

Love it or loathe it, you can't deny this grape its place in wine's hall of fame. Some of the very best examples hail from Burgundy, where texture, finesse, structure, and ageing ability rule over simple "drink-now" fruit flavours. You see, Chardonnay comes in all different shapes and sizes. Flavours range from the delicate, citrus, and slightly honeyed styles of Chablis to warmer, Southern-hemisphere styles, where aromas range from peaches and pears to full-throttle, ripe tropical fruits like banana, pineapple, guava, and mango.

Chenin Blanc
(shuh-nin blon)

Handier than a Swiss army knife, the globetrotting Chenin's high natural acidity and tendency to flirt with botrytis lend it equally well to a variety of styles: sweet, dry, or fizzy. A good traveller, Chenin's stomping ground is France's Loire Valley, where it makes racy dry whites, luscious sweet wines, and clean, frothy fizz. Expect aromas of apples, gooseberries, and fresh herbs.

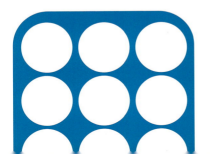

Gewurztraminer

(geh-verz-tra-mee-ner)

Like a drag queen with too much make-up and perfume (and little shame), this is the incredibly camp member of the white grape family. In reality, Gewurz is one of the superstar varieties of Alsace in France. The best ooze aromas of lychee, rose, orange blossom, cinnamon, ginger, and spice. Good Gewurz will be rich and weighty, with great length of flavour.

Marsanne

Clean, fresh, and fruity, this grape plays second fiddle to Viognier in France's northern Rhône Valley; however, it dominates many of the white wine blends of the southern Rhône. Expect ripe, peachy fruit flavours, fresh acidity, and barely a whiff of oak. With a bit of age, Marsanne takes on an amazing honeyed character and becomes slightly oilier, with more weight and richness. Outside France, you might see it in parts of Australia.

Muscat

For the purposes of this book, the large Muscat family of grapes can be split into non-identical triplets: Muscat Blanc à Petits Grains, Muscat of Alexandria, and Muscat Ottonel. Wine styles vary from light, fizzy Moscato d'Asti (northwest Italy) and sweet, spirity Muscat de Beaumes-de-Venise (France's Rhône Valley), to Spain's aromatic Málagas and the unique liqueur Muscats of Australia's northeast Victoria.

Palomino Fino

(pal-o-mee-no fee-no)

The most important variety in the production of sherry, accounting for four of the five main styles: manzanilla, fino, amontillado, and oloroso. Fino is the most popular and one of the greatest food wines in the world. The best are bone-dry, nutty, and slightly salty, with great mineral texture and a clean, tangy finish.

Pedro Ximénez
(pay-dro hee-may-neth)

Although "PX", as it's more commonly called, falls into the white grape family, this sun-loving variety produces sweet, thick, syrupy wines. Great examples are almost black in colour, viscous, and super-sweet, with intense aromas of raisin and spice.

Pinot Gris / Pinot Grigio
(pee-no gree/pee-no gree-jee-o)

Technically, these are the same grape; the key difference lies in the style. Pinot Grigio tends to be light, delicate, and fresh, usually made in stainless-steel tanks and best drunk young, when it's zippy and vibrant. Pinot Gris is fatter and richer, with more weight and intensity, often from time spent in oak. Pinot Grigio is commonly found in the cool of northeast Italy, while Pinot Gris is never more happy than in its classic "home", the French region of Alsace. There are also some fabulously aromatic examples emerging from New Zealand nowadays, perfect for fusion and Thai-style dishes, and shellfish too.

Riesling
(rees-ling)

Technically brilliant, but still a wee bit nerdy, Riesling currently represents some of this planet's great bargain wine buys. While its spiritual home is Germany, you'll find world-class examples from Austria, France, and Australia. The best will have beautiful, pure, citrus fruit aromas alongside fresh-cut flowers and spice, with flavours of lemons, limes, and minerals.

Sauvignon Blanc
(so-vin-yon blon)

Think passion-fruit, gooseberry, elderflower, blackcurrant… even cat's pee! France, South Africa, Chile, and Australia all have a good crack at it, but New Zealand (Marlborough, to be exact) has become the modern home of this variety. The best examples are pale, unmistakably pungent on the nose, painfully crisp, and ultra-refreshing with plenty of zip and racy acidity.

Semillon

(sem-ee-yon)

Sémillon is native to Bordeaux in France, but it's down under in New South Wales's Hunter Valley that Semillon (note the lack of accent on the "e") has had greatest success, producing beautifully crafted and insanely long-lived wines. In its youth, great examples explode with pear, white peach, and other ripe summer fruits. But stash a bottle away for a rainy day a few years down the line and you'll witness this variety's true magic: aromas of super-intense citrus fruit – even marmalade – alongside toast, honey, nuts, and sweet spice.

Sherry

Sherry is the English term for the wine-producing region of Jerez-de-la-Frontera in Spain's Andalucia. There are a number of styles produced in the sherry-producing triangle over there, and from a number of different varieties. Wine styles can run anywhere from bone-dry to super-sweet, while the key grape varieties used to produce them are Palomino Fino, Pedro Ximénez, and Moscatel.

Verdicchio

(vehr-dik-ee-o)

Verdicchio is grown and produced in Italy's central Marche region, and can make everything from light, crisp whites to big, rich ones. All are pretty neutral when it comes to aroma, but super-lemony in flavour, with the best showing plenty of spice and richness. Because of their weight, the full-bodied examples can handle oak too, so expect to see some wooded examples.

Viognier

(vee-on-yay)

Viognier overflows with intoxicating aromas of apricots, orange rind, and fresh-cut flowers. It's weighty, rich, and oily in texture, with great length and beautifully soft acidity. Native to France's northern Rhône, it also shows promise in Australia and South Africa.

The Reds

Cabernet Sauvignon
(kab-er-nay so-veen-yon)

King of the red grapes; the best display power, finesse, elegance, the ability to age, and universal appeal. Its home was Bordeaux, but particularly good examples now also come from Italy, Spain, Chile, Argentina, South Africa, Australia, and California. The range of flavours and aromas varies greatly, but look for blackcurrant, dark cherry, and plummy fruit alongside cedar, mint, and eucalyptus.

Carmenère
(car-men-yair)

Carmenère can be a nightmare in the vineyard: it's hard to get ripe, and once it is, you have a tiny window in which to pick it before the acidity disappears. But when it's good, it's really good! Bearing an uncanny likeness to Merlot, the best examples are bursting with super-dark fruits (plums, blackberries, and black cherries) and aromas of spice and leather.

Chianti
(ki-AN-tee)

Chianti is a region in Tuscany made up of eight distinct sub-districts, including the key ones of Colli Senesi, Classico, and Rufina. It circles the city of Florence and extends toward Sienna in the south. There are eight grape varieties permitted for use in Chianti, although few producers nowadays use all eight (some of which are white), with many preferring to focus on Tuscany's native red star, Sangiovese. Increasingly, Merlot, Cabernet Sauvignon, and Syrah are being used to "bulk up" Sangiovese's often lean and skeletal frame.

Grenache
(grin-ash)

Grown widely in Spain, France, and Australia, Grenache is the workhorse of red grapes, and can be a stand-alone performer in its own right. As concentrated, weighty, fully-fledged reds (especially in France's southern Rhône), the wines sit comfortably alongside some of the world's greatest. Grenache also provides the base for many rosés: its low tannin, acidity, and good whack of alcohol go perfect in pink.

Malbec

This red grape variety loves the sun and is found in Argentina's Andes Mountains (home to a handful of the highest-altitude vineyards on earth). These are often big wines, and the best are soft and super-fruity, with fantastically perfumed aromas of violets and lavender along with plenty of plums and spice.

Merlot

(mer-low)

Merlot has long played second fiddle to Big Brother Cabernet, often sidelined for blending. Yet it's the most widely planted red grape in Bordeaux, and in recent times both California and Australia have developed a love affair with it. New World examples tend to be plump, with ripe, plummy fruit and naturally low tannin. Wines from north of the equator are drier, leaner, and generally less in your face.

Mourvèdre

(more-ved-rah)

The star of the southern Rhône. Along with dark, sweet fruit there's mushroom, tobacco, roast lamb – even the elephant pen at the zoo! In Spain it's known as Monastrell and Mataró, while in Australia it's also known as Mataro. Because of its funkiness, it rarely appears solo and is usually reserved for blending.

Nebbiolo

(neb-ee-yo-lo)

The best examples of Nebbiolo are layered and complex, oozing aromas of tar, roses, dark cherry, black olives, and rosemary. In great wines, concentrated fruit, firm acidity, and a wash of drying tannins ensure that they'll go the distance if you want to stash them away. Nebbiolo's home is Piedmont, where it stacks up to everything, from mushrooms to chicken, rabbit, all sorts of game – even good old, mouldy cheeses.

Pinot Noir

(pee-no nwar)

Top examples of Pinot are seductive, intriguing, even sexy, and their versatility with food is near unrivalled. Thought of as one of the lightest reds, top examples show layers of strawberry, raspberry, plum, and dark forest fruits, with aromas of earth, spice, animal, cedar, and truffle. These wines range from delicate and minerally to silky and rich. Try those from the Côte de Nuits (Burgundy), and New Zealand's Central Otago and Martinborough regions.

Primitivo / Zinfandel

(prim-i-tee-vo / zin-fvan-del)

For ages we thought these were different varieties, but they're actually the same. Zinfandel ("Zin" for short) is found in the mighty USA, where most things big are seen as beautiful. In southern Italy, Primitivo rides high alongside Negroamaro and Nero d'Avola. With plenty of sweet, ripe fruit and aromas of violets and leather, this style is much more restrained than its transatlantic brother.

Rioja

(ree-O-hah)

Rioja in northern Spain is best known for its rich, full-flavoured reds. Tempranillo is the star grape, although red varieties Garnacha, Graciano, and Mazuelo are also permitted in the blend. Similarly, as a changing of the guard takes place, international varieties such as Cabernet Sauvignon, Merlot, and Syrah are increasingly finding their way into Rioja's modern face.

Rosé

(rose-AY)

It seems everyone has caught onto Rosé's food-friendliness and thirst-slaking credentials. Ranging from palest pink to almost garnet in colour, it can be made sweet, dry, or anywhere in between from just about any red grape. The most common way to make good rosé is called the *saignée* method. A bit like making a cup of tea, the skins are left in contact with the juice before fermentation to get the desired level of colour, flavour, and tannin. While Provence is making a comeback and California is holding its own, great rosés are emerging from Australia, South America, Spain, and Portugal. Even England has produced some fine examples.

Sangiovese

(san-gee-o-vay-zay)

Loaded with aromas of dark cherry, plum, and forest fruits, Sangiovese often also smells of tobacco, spice, and earth. Most remember its trademark "super-drying" tannins, which, without food, can make this grape a hard slog. It's native to Tuscany, where it shines as Chianti Classico and Brunello di Montalcino. More recently, it has surfaced in both Australia and the USA, but so far without the same success.

Syrah / Shiraz

(sih-rah/sheer-az)

Syrah is the French name for this grape. The style tends to be lighter in body than Shiraz, with aromas of redcurrants, raspberry, plum, and nearly always white pepper and spice. Shiraz, from Australia and the New World, tends to be concentrated and ripe. At its best, it oozes plum, raspberry, earth, cedar, and freshly ground black pepper. Some New World winemakers are now calling their wines Syrah to reflect the lighter style they are currently making.

Tempranillo

(tem-pra-nee-yo)

The grand old man of Spanish wine. Native to Rioja, it has also sunk its roots in nearby Ribera del Duero, Navarra, Priorat, and Toro. Typically, it has a solid core of dark berry fruits complete with a rustic edge that relies on savoury aromas such as tobacco, spice, leather, and earth. A recent trend has been to make international styles with big colour, big fruit, and big oak.

Touriga Nacional

(too-ree-ga na-ssee-o-nahl)

Touriga plays a starring role in many of Portugal's great fortified wines as well as being a key component in more than a few of its new-wave table wines. Deep, densely fruited, leathery, and with an almost inky texture, Touriga needs time to mellow. Expect to smell dried fruit, leather, and violets, while fortified wines will be richer, stacked with dried-fruit flavour, and boasting much sweetness.

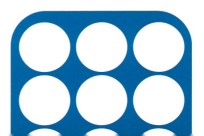

THE HOT
100

Skint

Drink

Dine •

Splurge

```
                                                I
                                             0
                                          9.4
                                       4.49
                                    5.99D
                                 0.69
                              0.99
                           1.69*
                        0.99

SECANO PIN/NOIR
CHAT/NEUF CLOS
1PT ORG ENG SS
SP CHIANTI CLAS
WD/HAVEN SHIRAZ                          44.27
DOM DE VERLAQUE
8 CRUMPETS
JUST A TASTE W
25CL LIEBFRAU
JUST A TASTE R

00414524
00190039
00971263
00104968
00437035
00423625
00182188
00264082
00263030
00264099

Total before saving

Still Wines Buy 4 Save 10%
  10% Discount

Balance to pay 10

Card tender

VISA C
CAR
```

25 wines for less

When money's tight, you make sacrifices. You start by trading in your gym membership, you continue by making your morning coffee at home rather than buying it out, those shoes you'd planned to throw away you fix, and the £6 you used to spend on a bottle of wine will soon enough become £4. This chapter lifts the lid on the best wines for as little money as possible. From a spread of countries, regions, varieties, and styles, these are simple wines for Tuesday nights in front of the telly, wines for bringing in the weekend, wines for lazy Sunday afternoons – wines that will soon enough have you saving your travel money and walking to work instead.

Skint

Penfolds Koonunga Hill Shiraz/Cabernet 2008

Multi-district blend
Australia

Love Will Keep Us Together by Captain & Tennille – Record of the Year in 1976, and more than just a little bit fitting, given that '76 was also the year Penfolds introduced its now much-loved Koonunga Hill Shiraz/Cabernet. In the 30-odd years since the Koonunga Hill brand has effortlessly juggled quality with value, it has grown to become the measuring stick for keenly priced reds everywhere.

A near equal-parts split of Shiraz and Cabernet Sauvignon styled around fruit from the South Australian districts of Barossa, McLaren Vale, and Coonawarra, among others, this wine remains beautifully fruited, sparingly oaked, and a great starting point for what Penfolds do incredibly well.

get it from...

£7.99

Sainsbury's
Waitrose
Fosters EMEA

Oxford Landing GSM 2007
Multi-district blend
South Australia

Oh la la! Like Paul Hogan in Lacoste, this straightforward Rhône-a-like blend of Grenache, Shiraz, and Mourvèdre is one of a growing number of its kind and, more importantly, a real breath of fresh air in the often-dreary world of cut-price wine. What makes it even better is the less-is-more approach that sees select parcels of the varieties mentioned above carefully blended to create a medium-bodied, fruit-rich wine minus the influence of oak – a wine that's as happy with food as without. If you need any more convincing, production is overseen by the good folk behind the controls at Yalumba.

get it from...

£6.20

Sainsbury's
Booths
Tanners Wine Merchants
Free Run Juice
Negociants UK

Jacob's Creek Riesling 2009 Barossa Valley Australia

Riesling lovers take note. As your favourite white grape gets more popular and more expensive by the minute – and more or less in that order – know that there's still a handful of super-affordable options out there that are well and truly worth a go. This would be one of them.

A translucent green/gold colour gets the box ticking off to a good start. It continues with a pure and compact nose of fresh limes and summer flowers. In your mouth it's incredibly well balanced, with textbook citrus zing and a long, dry finish wrapping things up nicely.

get it from...

£6.79

Tesco
Sainsbury's
Waitrose
Morrisons
Pernod Ricard UK

Mezzomondo Negroamaro 2008 Puglia Italy

Italy's wine-producing south has been on the rise for more than just a few years now. Sicily, Sardinia, Campania, and Puglia are not only producing consistently great wines but they are introducing us to a raft of new varieties such as Negroamaro. There's a whole lot to love about this value-packed Puglian red from the south-eastern subregion of Salento, otherwise known as "the heel" in Italy's boot.

With Negroamaro (black bitter) the star of the show, expect to find a nose flooded with black-berried fruit, liquorice, and cola aromas, while in your mouth it's flavour-packed, soft, a little bit chewy, and utterly delicious. At this price, is there a better partner to Friday night pizza? Surely not.

get it from...

£5.99

Waitrose

Constellation

Nepenthe
Adelaide Hills
Sauvignon Blanc 2009
Adelaide Hills
Australia

As great-value examples of Sauvignon Blanc continue to join the endangered-species list at an alarming rate of knots, its nice to know that a couple of Aussie offerings continue to fly the flag for the frugal.

Nepenthe is a much-loved producer from South Australia's Adelaide Hills, and with value-for-money, cool-climate wines like this, it's not hard to see why. Full of bounce, expect a nose loaded with blackcurrant, spring peas, and soft green herbs, while the palate is fresh as a daisy with bright tropical fruit and mouth-watering acidity.

get it from...

£8.99

The Co-op

Waitrose

Majestic Wine Warehouse

Australian Vintage Ltd

Yalumba
Y Series
Merlot 2007
Barossa Valley
Australia

Despite what was said about this variety in the cult wine flick *Sideways*, we still love Merlot. And how could you not? Good Merlot is like the vinous equivalent of a bear hug from your favourite Nana. And that's pretty special. Taking price into account, Yalumba do this variety better than most.

Pure purple colour extends to a deeply fruited nose of blood plums, leather, and chocolate, while in your mouth it's marshmallow-soft and supported beautifully by a wave of fine-grained tannins, minimal oak influence, and superb length of flavour.

get it from...

£7.71

House of Fraser
Cambridge Wine Cellar
Rhythm & Booze
Negociants UK

Wirra Wirra Scrubby Rise Shiraz/Cabernet/ Petit Verdot 2008 McLaren Vale Australia

In the bizarre and increasingly ridiculous world of made-up wine names, you'll be pleased to hear that Scrubby Rise is indeed a real place – a vineyard even. Possibly you couldn't care less, but whichever camp you fall into, seasoned bargain hunters will unanimously agree that the three wines that make up the Scrubby Rise range represent insane value for money.

The sole red is a medium-bodied blend of Shiraz and Cabernet Sauvignon that's been supercharged by a small shot of Petit Verdot. In both smell and taste, dark, sweet fruit is the message, with no obvious oak and a wash of dry, grainy tannins to finish things off.

get it from...

£8.45

Stevens Garnier

Support green

Whenever possible buy organic, biodynamic, and Fairtrade wines. Do a bit of research to find out who is doing what, or ask at your local wine shop, since many producers don't make mention of their green initiatives on their labels. Support those who are making an effort to leave the planet in better shape than they found it.

Jacob's Creek
Three Vines Rosé 2008
Barossa Valley
Australia

From the raft of great-value rosés that I have tasted this year, this would easily go down as one of the best. Even taking price into consideration, this three-way blend of Shiraz, Grenache, and Sangiovese is just jawdropping value for money.

Ultra-fresh, expect a nose of bright and aromatic red-berried fruit minus the bubble gum and confectionery aromas that hamper many New World offerings. The palate is clean as a whistle with more of those restrained red fruits, while drying tannin on the finish comes courtesy of the Sangiovese component.

get it from...
£6.99

Tesco
Asda
Budgens
Spar
Pernod Ricard UK

Peter Lehmann Clancy's Red 2006 Barossa Valley Australia

On the subject of great-value drinking, it would be remiss of me not to mention a wine that, despite its more-than-reasonable price tag, has been included in *Wine Spectator*'s Top 100 on no less than four occasions. With access to some of the best old vineyards in the Barossa Valley, Peter Lehmann's Clancy's combines Shiraz, Cabernet Sauvignon, and Merlot with a dash of Cabernet Franc to deliver a soft, plush, fruit-driven red that is designed for early consumption. In the winery, fermentation on skins lasts around seven days, prior to the wine being processed, clarified, and then matured in a combination of French and American oak for around 12 months.

get it from...

£7.99

Tesco
Waitrose
Oddbins
Peter Lehmann UK

Chivite
Gran Feudo
Rosado 2008
Navarra
Spain

As all-time wine bargains go, this is one of the best. For millions of years (okay, so not millions of years, but a long time nevertheless) Chivite has produced this bright-as-a-button, fruit-driven rosé from high up in Spain's northeast corner, where drinking rosé is as macho as running with bulls.

Like most examples from Navarra, Grenache is the star of this show and provides both the framework and the appropriate stuffing required to produce delicious rosé. Smells and flavours range from raspberry and wild strawberry through to ripe red apples and spice, all of which are nicely supported by a lick of tannin and a snappy, drying finish.

get it from...

£6.49

Waitrose
Oddbins
Weavers of Nottingham

TOP 20 TIPS
#**02**

Do your bit

Unless you're in the market for a
box of wine, ride your bike to your
local wine shop or – better still – walk.
Driving any more than a couple of
miles in your car uses up more CO_2
than shipping a bottle of wine from
Australia to the UK.

Rustenberg Brampton Shiraz 2006 Stellenbosch South Africa

Looking well beyond Chenin Blanc and Pinotage, South Africa's new breed is currently putting a number of alternative varieties through their paces. Most exciting in my opinion are the Rhône varietals – and this delicious all-terrain red from the talented Adi Badenhorst is a cracking example of exactly that.

Shiraz is only 90 per cent of the story here. Laying the foundation with all that lovely dark-red fruit, chocolate, and spice character, two per cent Viognier is co-fermented with the Shiraz to aid texture and aromatic lift, while around eight per cent Mourvèdre is blended into the finished wine, adding that ever-so-slightly rustic edge.

get it from...

£9.00

Hedley Wright Wine Merchants

The Great Grog Company

York Wines

Seckford Wines

Banrock Station Sparkling Shiraz NV
Multi-district blend Australia

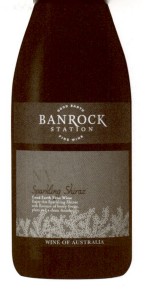

I appreciate that most people have absolutely no idea what to do with sparkling red wine – and to be honest, I'm not entirely sure myself, although I do know that apart from being firmly ingrained in Aussie Christmas culture (except no elder was able to confirm why), it's also the ultimate drink for Peking Duck.

Banrock Station produces one of the best-value and most reliable examples of this style known to man. Almost black to look at, expect an intense nose of blackberry jam and dark-bitter chocolate, while in your mouth it's sweet and intense, with balanced fizz and just the right amount of tannin.

get it from...
£9.00

Waitrose
Somerfield
Wine Rack
Constellation

Château Guiot Rosé Costières de Nîmes 2008 Provence France

Sandwiched between the Languedoc, Provence, and the Rhône, the precariously stony soils of the Costières de Nîmes provide a near-perfect environment in which to grow grapes. Locals François and Sylvia Cornut run the much-loved 120-hectare Château Guiot, with François in charge of the vineyards and Sylvia the winery.

Grenache, Syrah, and Cinsault are the stars here, producing a lush, juicy red and one of only two rosés I'd consider walking over hot coals for. Encompassing all three varieties, expect a nose crammed with raspberry, redcurrant, and dried-herb aromas, while a fresh, fruity palate gives way to crunchy acidity and a clean, drying finish.

get it from...

£6.99

Majestic
Wine Warehouse

Four Sisters Sauvignon Blanc 2008
Multi-district blend Australia

Almost a dozen years ago, Trevor Mast – one of Australia's most knowledgeable and enduring winemakers – launched the Four Sisters range, receiving widespread praise in the process. Today it remains the best-value selection of its kind.

Select parcels of Sauvignon Blanc are drawn from a number of cool-climate regions in a bid to produce a bright, herbaceous style, and one that's geared for drinking a.s.a.p. Lean, tight, and well structured, the nose is loaded with smells of passion-fruit, green apple, and mown grass, while in the mouth it's vibrant, zippy, and bone-dry.

get it from...

£7.99

Field & Fawcett
Wine Merchants
& Delicatessen

Cheers Bottle Shop

Redfield Wines

Dillons Wine Stores

Cotswold Vintners

Ehrmanns

Cellier des Dauphins Côtes du Rhône-Villages Vinsobres 2007
Southern Rhône France

A new injection of energy (and possibly cash) has seen the once-weary wines of the Cellier des Dauphins cooperative return to form. However, one wine in particular – a traditional blend of Grenache, Syrah, Mourvèdre, and Cinsault from the southern Rhône appellation of Vinsobres – grabbed my attention.

And at a snip under eight quid, it's a cracker. Delicious ripe raspberry fruit dominates the nose here alongside trademark aromas of southern Rhône bramble and spice. Time in oak is kept to a minimum, but there is enough fruit tannin on board to keep an otherwise amply fruited palate in check.

get it from...

£7.99

Waitrose

Vallis Mareni Ombra Prosecco NV Veneto Italy

Given the choice, a glass of really good Prosecco – of which there are few – is always a far better proposition than a really average glass of Champagne – of which there are far too many. Luckily, there has been a noticeable rise in the amount of good Prosecco coming forward, one of which is Ombra.

Prosecco grapes are fermented to form base wines, blended, and then refermented in large tanks prior to bottling under pressure. The result in this case is a clean, modern wine with aromas of lemon skin, green apple, and honeysuckle. The palate is softer and less gassy than most sparkling wines, and best of all it weighs in for a third of the price of most average Champagnes.

get it from...

£9.99

Oddbins
Virgin Wines
Revino

TOP 20 TIPS
#**03**

Shop
sensibly

PET, Tetra, and lightweight
glass are all better for
the environment. Do a bit
of research to find out
who is using them and
support those brands.

Brown Brothers Moscato 2009 King Valley Australia

I'm all for wines that make you smile, and no single wine style has the ability to make you smile quite like Moscato. Muscat of Alexandria – a grape variety that up until recently was about as popular as having a tooth pulled – has done the unthinkable and gone from ugly duckling to bona fide hottie almost overnight.

Brown Brothers' Moscato is just one of the many great local examples of this fresh summer style native to Italy's north-west. Fermented under pressure until it's just over five per cent ABV, expect aromas of fresh grape juice, ripe pear, and juicy red apples, while in your mouth it's squeaky clean, a little bit sweet, and ever so slightly fizzy.

get it from...

£4.99

Tesco (selected stores)
Brown Brothers Europe

Doña Dominga Old Vines Chardonnay / Semillon 2009 Colchagua Chile

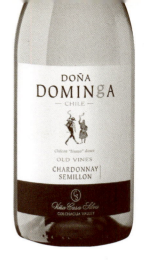

Chardonnay has had a makeover. Gone, in most cases, is the heavy-handed use of oak, the super-sized tropical fruit, and the everything-but-the-kitchen-sink approach to winemaking that put so many of you off to begin with. The new face of Chardonnay is leaner and more focused, and as a result, wines are not only better balanced but better suited to food too.

Which leads me to a Sunday lunch favourite. Piping hot oven aside, a whole chicken stuffed with lemon, butter, garlic, salt, pepper, and fresh thyme is all you need to create Chardonnay heaven. You'll need rich, sweet fruit and spicy oak to match the flavour of the bird, you'll need weight and length to carry flavour, and you'll need focused acidity to cut through fat and clean your palate. This cracking example from Doña Dominga incorporates a small shot of Semillon to keep things daisy-fresh.

get it from...

£5.99

Oddbins
Thierry's

Torres
Sangre de Toro
2007
Penedès
Spain

I've been telling you for many moons about the great value that is Sangre de Toro. For decades this delicious little wine from Spain's north east corner has been winning hearts right around the globe for its uncomplicated, easy-drinking style and, dare I say it, for that little black plastic bull that comes attached to the neck of every bottle – which kind of makes it like the adult equivalent of a Kinder Surprise chocolate egg.

This straightforward blend of Garnacha and Cariñena minus the influence of oak is rich with aromas of raspberry, smoke, and spice. The palate is soft, forward, and provides delicious everyday drinking – hands down one of the absolute bargains of the year.

get it from...

£5.99

Sainsbury's
Morrisons
Asda
Booths
Thresher
J E Fells & Sons

Quinta da Bacalhao Tinto da Anfora 2007
Alentejo Portugal

Portugal's new wave of dry red table wines has created serious buzz on a number of fronts, particularly in the value-for-money stakes. From the hot and barren Alentejo in south-central Portugal, this is a cracking example of the new wave, and a wine that drinks beautifully right now.

Tinto da Anfora is a dark and chewy blend of Castelão, Trincadeira, and Aragonez (a.k.a. Tempranillo) – among other things – that comes sporting masses of dark dried fruit, smoke, and spice on the nose, while in your mouth it's inky and full. Bright acidity, cedary oak, and fine, chewy tannins complete the picture.

get it from...

£6.49

Sainsbury's

Waitrose

Majestic
Wine Warehouse

TOP 20 TIPS

#**04**

Drink
local

Wines from local
vineyards have had
to travel less.
This is a good thing.

Concha y Toro
Late Harvest
Sauvignon Blanc 2006
Maule Valley
Chile

I'm a sucker for a good pavlova and fortunately my mother-in-law makes one of the best. It comes with a thick meringue base about the size of a 12-inch record, followed by a layer of cream, and then another slightly smaller layer of meringue, more cream, and finally an explosion of fresh passion-fruit pulp and big, sweet strawberry halves. It's a sight to behold – but nowhere near as impressive as the spectacle of me trying to force a slice into my gob. Fortunately, suitable wine matches are in abundance and this cracker from Chilean powerhouse Concha y Toro is perfect.

On the nose expect pretty pineapple, honey, and candied citrus fruits, while in your mouth it's fresh – not at all cloying – clean, and lively, with great concentration and length.

get it from...

£5.99 (50cl)

Booths
Oddbins
Majestic Wine Warehouse
Harrods
Concha y Toro UK

Cono Sur Reserve Merlot 2008 Colchagua Valley Chile

As a company, Cono Sur is an unashamedly environmentally conscious modernist on a mission to produce the very best wines possible from a spread of regions. Merlot mainly, but with small additions of Malbec, Cabernet Sauvignon, Syrah, and Alicante Bouschet, grapes are taken from the clay-rich soils of Colchagua Valley where long, warm days become long, cool nights, providing just the kind of conditions in which Merlot thrives.

Expect masses of dark, sun-drenched fruit and spice on the nose, while a mouthful will reveal a lush, inky wave of sweet fruit, spicy new oak, and a wash of dry, grippy tannins. All grapes are hand-harvested and, post fermentation, 60 per cent of the wine is matured in barrel for a period of ten months.

get it from...

£7.99

Booths

Oddbins

Majestic Wine Warehouse

Harrods

Concha y Toro UK

Share your wine

Drink wine with other people. Get a group of friends together, open a whole load of bottles, plonk them in the middle of the table, taste, talk, listen, and laugh – it's another great way to learn about wine.

Paul Mas Estate Marsanne Vin de Pays d'Oc 2008 Languedoc France

The wines of dynamic Languedoc producer Paul Mas have raised more than their fair share of eyebrows in recent times. Not only are they well made and great value-for-money but many are also from less-than-popular grape varieties. Take Marsanne, for example. When was the last time you bought a bottle of Marsanne? Exactly.

This is a cracking example – richer than the handful of others I've tried over the past year – where bright stone fruit, honey, and nutty oak are offset by lively acidity, all of which results in the kind of wine that drinks beautifully now, but might just drink better in two or three years' time. Not something you see everyday at this price.

get it from...

£7.99

Majestic
Wine Warehouse

Casillero del Diablo
Shiraz Rosé 2008
Central Valley
Chile

Chile is working overtime to shake off its "cheap and cheerful" reputation, with the production of some breathtaking wines from cooler regions. Still, Chile does cheap and cheerful better than just about anybody, and so for that reason – much as we're excited by the advances being made – we hope they never completely lose the ability to produce the cracking bargains they do.

This full-throttle dry rosé from Chilean juggernaut Concha y Toro boasts deep colour with plenty of dark-berried fruit and subtle spice, both of which are nicely supported by a lick of tannin and cleansing acidity.

get it from...

£6.99

Tesco
Sainsbury's
Waitrose
Thresher
Concha y Toro UK

Dom Brial
Muscat de Rivesaltes
2007
Midi
France

Muscat *vin doux naturel* (VDN) is made using the process of *mutage* – otherwise known as fortification – the adding of neutral grape spirit (96 per cent ABV) to the fermenting must, giving a "naturally" sweet wine with 100–125 grams per litre of residual sugar and around 15 per cent of alcohol.

With 380 members cultivating around 2,100 hectares, La Cave des Vignerons de Baixas is a modern cooperative selling VDN wines under the label Dom Brial, after a Benedictine monk who introduced the court of Louis XVI to the local wines. Expect a lush and highly aromatic nose of dried apricot, honey, and candied oranges leading to a clean and spirity palate with sweet, mouth-filling fruit and great length of flavour.

get it from...

£8.99 (50cl)

Waitrose
Hennings Wine Merchants
Vinology
Daniel Lambert Wines

25 wines for food

Food glorious food, and made even better in this chapter by well-chosen wine. Like a romantic night in with your better half, food and wine matching shouldn't be an exercise wheeled out only on special occasions, and nor does it need to be expensive or time consuming. Some of the best combinations are also some of the cheapest and easiest to reproduce. And whether you choose to follow the rules or break them all, at the very heart of it, good food and wine matching knits a little bit of art with a little bit of science and a lot of trial and error. Practice makes perfect – *bon appétit*!

Altos Las Hormigas Malbec 2008 Mendoza Argentina

Tough times call for tough measures – which if you're a carnivore might mean rethinking your favourite cut of meat. Beef-lovers who don't mind a bit of a chew should consider the skirt, the rump, or brisket – all of which pack plenty of flavour at a fraction of the cost.

Grill it simply over coals if you can, or in the pan if you can't, and serve with nothing more than a drizzle of good olive oil, a pinch of sea salt, and a dollop of your favourite mustard. The rugged and user-friendly Altos Las Hormigas Malbec is the ideal sparring partner, with layer upon layer of sweet, dark fruit leading to a full-bodied palate where fruit and oak coexist happily. Dry, grippy tannins will help reduce the chew-factor no end.

get it from...

£8.99

Noel Young Wines

Whole Foods Market

WoodWinters
Wines & Whiskies

Liberty Wines

Wither Hills
Sauvignon Blanc
2008
Marlborough
New Zealand

Sauvignon Blanc – particularly the Kiwi kind – is perfectly geared toward the flavours of spring, and you would struggle to find a more spring-like dish than spaghetti tossed with the first of the season's broad beans, peas, mint, basil, and a good squeeze of lemon.

Wither Hills produce a cracking example of the Kiwi kind that's both widely available and really good value for money. Pale and pungent, expect plenty of personality with aromas of passion-fruit, gooseberry, lime-flavoured lollies, and soft green herbs, while in your mouth it's intense – packed with all of the above – and beautifully balanced by focused natural acidity.

get it from...
£8.99

Tesco
The Co-op
Waitrose
Oddbins
Bibendum Wine

Celler de Capçanes Mas Collet 2006
Tarragona Spain

Celler de Capçanes is a reinvigorated co-op in the northern Spanish region of Montsant. Refreshingly, and in stark contrast to many of the wines from neighbouring Priorat, a number of local wines come across as pure, unadulterated – and affordable.

Old-vine Garnacha, Tempranillo, Cariñena, and Cabernet Sauvignon combine to form a soft, spicy red that is perfectly suited to char-grilled lamb cutlets dusted with dry-ground Middle Eastern spices such as cinnamon, coriander seed, cumin, fennel seed, mustard seed, cardamom, and star anise. Two minutes each side over a smoking hot barbecue together with a pot of minted yoghurt for dipping will do the trick nicely.

get it from...
£7.99

Waitrose

Booths

Swig

D Byrne & Co

Gauntleys of Nottingham

Vinites

Taltarni Clover Hill Brut 2005 Tasmania Australia

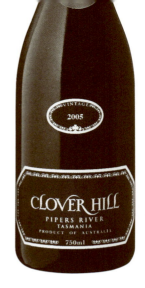

It doesn't take much to mash a few potatoes together with some flaked white fish. Add a handful of chopped parsley, a few salty capers, brush with egg, roll in breadcrumbs and – presto! – fish cakes ready for a hot pan. Bubbles are your best bet here, and Taltarni Clover Hill is among the finest sparkling wines produced outside the boundaries of Champagne.

From the word go there is a lovely nose of rich citrus fruit, fresh baked bread, and spice. The palate is oh so long with plenty of mouth-filling fruit and a wash of fine, tiny bubbles to finish. If there's a party in the offing, roll the fish cakes golf ball size and serve them golden and crunchy with plenty of garlicky aioli for dipping.

get it from...

£16.50

Oddbins
Planet of the Grapes
DeFINE Food & Wine
Alliance Wines

Catena Alamos Chardonnay 2007 Mendoza Argentina

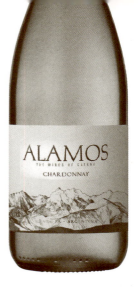

The luxurious suckling pig is one of those versatile wine dishes that can go either way. Its sweet, tender meat and salty crackling are perfectly suited to a range of medium-bodied, dry, grippy reds, or equally at home with a cast of full-flavoured spicy whites. As a die-hard Chardonnay fan, I'm always up for option B.

Tucked neatly into the foothills of the Andes Mountains, Argentine powerhouse Catena produces a brilliant style of Chardonnay that speaks volumes about texture, finesse, elegance, and structure, and, most importantly, without leaving you feeling as though you've been gnawing on a piece of timber. Aromas here are of grapefruit, marzipan, and cashew, while in your mouth it's incredibly long, full, spicy, and dry.

get it from...

£7.99

Majestic
Wine Warehouse

Noel Young Wines

Hailsham Cellars

Bibendum Wine

Mount Langi Ghiran Billi Billi Shiraz 2005
Great Western Australia

If you know of a good Italian deli, then chances are that somewhere tucked away in among the labyrinth of olive oil, cured meat, olives, dried pasta, and nougat coated in dark chocolate will be the classic pork, fennel, and chilli sausage. Like most things in Italy, everyone has a slightly different take on these sausages, but taste a good one straight from the barbecue and you'll be hooked.

Once a week I drive an hour across town for mine. And to drink? Ranking third in the Mount Langi tier of quality, it's hard to go past the super-priced Billi Billi – a soft, forward-drinking example of cool-climate Shiraz loaded with sweet berryish fruit and plenty of fresh ground pepper character – perfect with your bangers.

get it from...

£7.99

Majestic Wine Warehouse

The Wine Society

The Sussex Wine Company

Hic Wines

Enotria Winecellars

Do things by halves

Half bottles can often provide some amazing value, not to mention the fact that they mature more quickly than a full bottle. Half bottles are also a great alternative to buying wines by the glass, which can often suffer after the pouring bottle has been open for a while.

Hugel
Pinot Blanc 2007
Alsace
France

Saturday lunch in our house is about recycling. All the leftovers from the last week get a quick spruce before being served on a huge plate in help-yourself fashion. On any given Saturday you'll find some bizarre configuration of olives, caperberries, anchovies, ham, salami, a couple of tomatoes from the garden, chickpeas, avocado, feta, and baba ganoush, and always together with plenty of crusty bread.

A couple of glasses of wine and the Saturday papers make it far more civilized, and this perennial favourite from Hugel is bang on the money. Clean and crisp with a nose full of pear, lemon, and honey-suckle character; in your mouth it's soft and delicate with moderate acidity and a long, drying finish – the perfect precursor to a lazy Saturday nap on the couch.

get it from...

£9.49

Bentalls

Lewis & Cooper

J E Fells & Sons

Perrin & Fils Cairanne Côtes du Rhône Villages 2008 Southern Rhône France

Take it from me. The odd token bottle of wine goes a long way with most good butchers. Far enough that in many cases they'll not only happily cut you multiple slices of wafer-thin veal escalope – an annoying job at the best of times – but happily offer to pound them flat for you too.

And that matters because the schnitzel is back, a dish that besides being ridiculously easy to produce (provided you've got a kind-natured butcher) is also really wine friendly. As a rule, medium-bodied reds with minimal oak will serve you best and this bright and breezy offering from Southern Rhône star Perrin would be spot on.

get it from...

£9.49

Waitrose

Unison
Rosé 2009
Hawke's Bay
New Zealand

As food-friendly wine styles go, rosé ranks right up there with the best of them. With the added advantage of being anything from light, heavy, sweet, dry, or somewhere in between, rosé can handle pretty much everything from a straightforward tomato salad right the way through to all the charred and sticky things that the barbecue can manage. That said, the freshest mozzarella you can lay your hands on paired with a couple of slices of sweet Parma ham and a drizzle of good olive oil is one of the best, and easiest, matches for light, dry rosé you can produce.

Hawke's Bay star Unison produces a dry and full-bodied style of rosé from a mixture of Syrah, Merlot, and Cabernet Sauvignon. There's plenty of fresh fruit on board backed up by the faintest lick of tannin and balanced acidity to match.

get it from...

£12.95

Wimbledon Wine Cellar

New Zealand Wine Distribution Co

TOP 20 TIPS
#**07**

Ask away

Ask your sommelier. Ask the
girl behind the counter of your
local wine store. Ask the guy
at the winery. No matter how
stupid you think your questions
may be, ask away. This is how
you will learn more about wine.

Warre's Warrior Port Wine Reserve NV
Douro
Portugal

As the fortified market continues to flounder amid changing tastes and out-of-date marketing, please make a note that this is delicious port for just a snip under a tenner a bottle. Maybe one of the best. It also comes with a decent CV, having been shipped continuously since the 1750s, making Warrior the oldest and most consistent port brand currently doing battle.

Unfiltered and having been matured in oak for an extended period prior to release, this is concentrated and power-packed port with a nose of dried fig, dark plum, and bitter chocolate. In your mouth it's inky and rich, with masses of intensity and a clean, beautifully balanced finish.

get it from...

£8.99

Tesco
Sainsbury's
Asda
Waitrose
J E Fells & Sons

Willunga 100 McLaren Vale Cabernet/ Shiraz 2006 McLaren Vale South Australia

Cabernet Sauvignon, Shiraz, and lamb share an amazing relationship. Slow-roasted shoulder of lamb (rather than the more expensive leg) surrounded by winter veggies is a tried and tested classic, although to my mind there's nothing like the smell of lamb – rubbed with a mixture of garlic, rosemary, and sea salt – grilling over charcoal.

And whether you pan-fry, char-grill, or roast your meat, Shiraz's core of dark fruit should naturally knit with the sweet, earthy flavour of lamb, while trademark dry, grainy tannin from Cabernet's thick skins will work wonders at breaking down protein and cutting through fat. This example from Willunga 100 ranks as one of the best of its kind on the market.

get it from...

£7.99

Noel Young Wines
Wimbledon Wine Cellar
Markinch Wine Gallery
Liberty Wines

Quinta de Covela Escolha White 2008
Douro
Portugal

As Portugal continues its rapid ascent towards wine-producing greatness, this stunning white is a cracking illustration of the country's new breed. Having recently been inducted into the prestigious biodynamic group, La Renaissance des Appellations, Quinta de Covela prides itself on serious attention to detail in the vineyard.

As an eccentric and unoaked (identifiable by a silver capsule) blend of the native Avesso with Chardonnay and Gewurztraminer, expect ripe tropical fruit and spice on the nose, while in the mouth it's voluptuous, rich, and above all delicious. Smoked eel and cream of horseradish is a potent and full-flavoured combination made all the better with a wine such as this.

get it from...

£9.49

Waitrose

Champalou
Vouvray Sec Tendre 2007
Loire Valley
France

Together, Didier and Catherine Champalou produce some of the finest examples of Chenin Blanc to be found in the Loire Valley. Having established their property in 1984, and covering all bases from fizzy, to dry, to oak, to no oak, to sweet, and even sweeter, the Champalous have worked tirelessly to become known as one of the regions true shining lights.

From the dry camp, this is a delicious Vouvray, where a restrained nose of dried apple, honey, and minerals makes way for a palate that manages to be both rich and broad with real weight and intensity, yet without being flabby. Drinking beautifully now, but built to last.

get it from...
£10.95

Great Western Wine
Les Caves de Pyrene
Enotria Winecellars

Fonseca
Crusted Port NV
Douro
Portugal

Good wine and cheese matches aren't as difficult to produce as you might imagine, largely because you're combining two finished products. Firstly, consider texture, balancing the weight of your wine and cheese as evenly as possible. Also consider flavour – generally the more flavour you have in your cheese, the more you'll need in your wine.

To this end, Port and Stilton make one of the all-time classic combinations, and this great example from Fonseca – who have been turning out some of the regions finest examples since the eighteenth century and continue as the measuring stick of quality today – is perfect. Expect a deep and complex nose of dark spices, fruits, bitter chocolate, and nicely worn leather, while the palate blossoms into a plush, bittersweet, and delicious mouthful of wine.

get it from...

£15.00

Majestic
Wine Warehouse

Hailsham Cellars

Giles de Maré

Mentzendorff

Pewsey Vale
Prima Riesling 2008
Eden Valley
Australia

Whole deep-fried bass with green papaya salad would come extremely close to being my desert-island dish. Team it with a glass of Germanic-style Pewsey Vale Prima Riesling and it would most likely win hands down. Where most European cooking proves pretty straightforward for wine matching, Southeast Asian cookery definitely does not.

With palm sugar, lime juice, fish sauce, and those numbingly hot little bird's eye chillies (that's sweet, sour, salty, and hot all in one go) forming the basis for many Thai salads, you can probably appreciate that few wine styles are up to the job. Riesling is the exception. Look for examples with some degree of sweetness. This will help you account for most of the hurdles. And as a word of warning to chilli fanatics like me, be wary of how much chilli you use in your cooking – even the most suitable wines have their limits.

get it from...

£10.65

Noel Young Wines

Hoults Wine Merchants

Hailsham Cellars

Hanging Ditch Wine Merchants

Negociants UK

Planeta
Rosé 2008
Sicily
Italy

There's freshness to Sicilian food that, no matter where you are or how cold it may be, literally makes you want to pick up your plate and move outside. In short, this is food that reminds you of eating outdoors – food that reminds you of summer.

Start with a couple of squares of sheeps' milk ricotta, and then for the salad combine a couple of small, sweet tomatoes halved and then quartered, a few salted capers, black olives, a handful each of fresh coriander and spearmint leaves, then a few drops of red wine vinegar, a pinch of sea salt, and good olive oil to finish. Planeta Rosato 2008 is the perfect partner. Made from 100 per cent Syrah and sourced from Sicily's north-west corner, it is fruit-fresh and bone dry, and outstanding value for money.

get it from...

£11.50

Swig
Enotria Winecellars

TOP 20 TIPS
#**08**

Wine is for drinking

It's easy to fall into the trap of buying wine to keep and then never getting around to drinking it before it starts its downward slide. Don't get too precious about your bottles – open and share them.

Raventós i Blanc L'Hereu Reserva Brut 2007 Penedès Spain

Having been passed down from generation to generation since 1497, the skills and knowledge that go into Raventós i Blanc are unsurpassed. This engaging winery produces clean and forward wines that combine the best of the old and the new. Like many of Cava's best producers, efforts are focused on the vineyards in a bid to yield the best fruit possible.

Assembled from the traditional blend of Macabeo (60 per cent), Parellada (20 per cent) and Xarel-lo (20 per cent) expect to find a compact wine concealing plenty of bright green apple and lemon sherbet character. In your mouth there is soft stone and citrus fruit flavor, while a charge of tiny bubbles balances things out nicely. The perfect aperitif, or equally brilliant with a dozen natural oysters.

get it from...

£15.00

Handford Wines

The Dorset Wine Company

Martinez Wines

Hamilton Yorke & Co

Domaine la Roubine Côtes du Rhône Sablet 2006 Southern Rhône France

Up the road from Gigondas is Sablet – a tiny commune with deep, sandy soils that makes slightly lighter wines than those of Gigondas, but from the same mix of varieties.

Assembled from Grenache (80 per cent), Cinsault (10 per cent) – both of which were taken from 50-year-old vines – and Syrah (10 per cent), this gluggable, medium-bodied wine is loaded with bright raspberry and sour-cherry fruit and trademark Rhône pepper, and it happens to be drinking beautifully now. Fermentation lasts around six weeks and takes place in glass-lined concrete tanks. No oak is used in this *cuvée*.

get it from...

£9.95

Flint Wines

Louis Jadot Combe aux Jacques Beaujolais-Villages 2008 Burgundy France

The great Jacques Lardière has been handcrafting outstanding wines at Maison Louis Jadot in Burgundy for nearly 40 years. This includes some terrific wines from Beaujolais, most notably the utterly delicious Beaujolais-Villages Combe aux Jacques.

Bright, bouncy, and best served with a slight chill, this is top-drawer Gamay taken from the very best sites within the Beaujolais-Villages appellation. Expect to find a nose that explodes with liqueur cherry, violet, and spice aromas, while in your mouth it's soft, plush, and beautifully balanced by a wash of ultra-fine, drying tannins.

get it from...

£8.99

Tesco
Waitrose
Budgens
Booths
Hatch Mansfield

Leitz Rüdesheimer Riesling Kabinett 2008 Rheingau Germany

There is a recipe from food writer and über-cook Nigel Slater that has become a firm winter favourite in our house. It takes chunks of fatty pork belly and renders them down for hours with plenty of onions, butter, lemons, parsley, and capers. It's a completely delicious and sticky dish, even if it's just a tad unhealthy – a dish that's literally built for great Riesling.

From one of Germany's brightest young stars comes this textbook example of great modern Riesling. Fresh and limey with further aromas of sweet spice, ginger, and summer flowers. In the mouth it's delicate, just a little bit sweet, and beautifully balanced by mineral texture and super-fresh acidity. Don't attempt Nigel's pork-belly casserole without it!

get it from...

£9.49

Booths
Adnams Cellar & Kitchen
Villeneuve Wines
ABS Wine Agencies

Vesevo
Greco di Tufo 2008
Campania
Italy

Friday night is pizza night in the Skinner house. If we're feeling motivated we'll make them from scratch, covering the kitchen in flour as we go, otherwise we'll just ring them in. Whichever we choose, the topping combinations seem to stay pretty consistent: tomato, mozzarella, capers and anchovy, salami and fresh chilli, potato, and rosemary, or the tried and tested classic, the Margarita.

And yes, while we know the best pizza wines are usually red, this delicious white from the chilly hills of Campania is right up to the task. Pure and racy, with a nose that's rich with aromas of lemon, beeswax, and marzipan, while in your mouth expect rounded citrus fruit bound by lovely mineral texture.

get it from...

£11.99

Majestic
Wine Warehouse

Harvey Nichols

Valvona & Crolla

Liberty Wines

Serve it at the right temperature

More often than not we serve white wine too cool and red wine not cool enough. If wine is served at the wrong temperature, you risk changing the aromatics, the flavours, and the textures of a wine. And while 20 minutes in the freezer is okay, the microwave is definitely out of bounds.

Campbells
Rutherglen Muscat NV
Rutherglen
Australia

Australia's fortified wines are unique in the sense that they represent a little slice of liquid history. They're wines that have kept drinkers smiling for well in excess of 130 years, yet sadly they never quite get the consumer recognition they deserve. The process from start to finish is long and laborious, and finished wines are often left to mature for decades. Relative to the cost of production, Australia's fortified wines represent some of the wine world's last great bargains and some of the best things to drink with food.

This example sits atop a pile of truly mind-blowing Aussie fortifieds. With the constituent wines having an average age of 12 years, but drawing on blending material far older, this is pure and concentrated dried-raisin fruit, mocha, and exotic spice, complete with a beautifully textured palate, fresh acidity, and a long, sweet finish.

get it from...

£8.99 (37.5 cl)

Waitrose
Oddbins
ABS Wine Agencies

Yalumba
Botrytis Viognier 2007
Wrattonbully
Australia

Poached pears with really good ice-cream – one of those bulletproof desserts made all the better by a well-chosen wine to match. But you have to be a little bit careful – you'll need weight and richness, and nothing too cloying. Viognier would be a good place to start. From dry all the way through to sweet, Yalumba do Viognier better than most, and this example is no exception.

This is a clean, modern style where aromas of citrus marmalade, apricot, and pineapple dominate, while in your mouth you can expect incredible length of flavour, a little alcoholic heat, and lovely bright acidity to tie things up.

get it from...

£10.20 (37.5 cl)

Australian Wines Online
Hermitage Cellars
Le Pont de la Tour
Whole Foods Market
Negociants UK

Château du Rouët Teres 2008
Provence France

Taylor's Automatic Refresher is a little pit stop in the Napa Valley renowned for the quality of their fish tacos. For your trouble you get two small, soft corn tortillas in which you find a couple of finger-sized strips of battered fish, fresh salsa and guacamole, and finished with a big squeeze of fresh lime.

As a rule, clean, fresh, zippy whites and pinks – wines that combine tart, citrussy flavours with crisp acidity – will serve you best, and king of that breed would have to be fresh, summery rosés like this brilliant blend of 60 per cent Grenache and 40 per cent Syrah from Chateau du Rouët. Grapes are picked by hand, and the wine made by first bleeding off the juice following a short and cool skin maceration. Delicious!

get it from...

£7.99

Wines of the World

Let it breathe

With the exception of the classics,
few wines being produced today
need to breathe for a long time.
Having said that, get yourself a
decanter and decant everything;
all reds and most full-bodied whites
will benefit from a quick burst
of oxygen 10–15 minutes before
you plan to serve them.

d'Arenberg
The Stump Jump 2007
McLaren Vale
Australia

THE JUICE
AWARDS 2010
Bargain
of the year

In the days before fancy diesel-powered farm equipment, the stump jump was an all-terrain plough that had the ability to ride over stumps and tough eucalyptus roots without pause. Today it's more commonly associated with d'Arenberg's much-loved everyday sipper – a wine that ranks as one of the best-value reds from Australia.

Stump Jump is an all-terrain blend of unwooded bush vine Grenache (50 per cent), Shiraz (29 per cent), and Mourvèdre (21 per cent). Like other wines in the d'Arenberg range, production includes fermentation in head-down, open-top fermenters followed by gentle basket-pressing.

get it from...

£7.99

Bacchanalia

Fresh & Wild

Corks & Cases

The Bristol Wine Company

Bibendum Wine

25 wines for living

Friends are coming for dinner, you're celebrating a pay rise, there's a birthday that needs toasting, maybe it's a night out at your favourite local restaurant, a day at the races, a romantic picnic for two – whatever the occasion, you'll be better off with a decent bottle of wine on stand-by. In this chapter I shine the light on the wines that consistently over-deliver, given what they'll set you back. Great as they are, these aren't wines for hoarding under your bed, or treating like they're the last bottles you're ever going to own – these are wines for drinking now, and better still, for sharing.

Drink

Bonterra Viognier 2008 Mendocino/ Lake County California

When I dream of running away somewhere a little less hectic than real life, I often think of the postcard-like Bonterra, complete with its rolling green hills, its blanket of vines, and its fresh mountain air. Yes, that would do me nicely. Set on a lush 153 hectares in the Mendocino countryside, Bonterra has been handcrafting a range of organically farmed wines since 1987.

From the range, this is delicious Viognier made all the better by small additions of Rhône stable mates Marsanne and Rousanne. Expect a nose brimming with smells of pear, apricot, and fresh summer flowers. And while the palate displays incredible intensity of fruit, it isn't at all blowsy and has just the right amount of alcoholic slip.

get it from...

£9.99

Waitrose

Majestic
Wine Warehouse

Booths

Brown-Forman UK

Domäne Wachau Terrassen Grüner Veltliner 2008
Wachau Austria

Despite sounding like a gang of well-to-do kids from Primrose Hill, the Bohemian Massif is in fact one of the oldest and most important geological rock formations in Austria. Over many millions of years, pressure and heat have impacted on the remnants of this prehistoric mountain range to form the current subsoil of the Wachau. As a result, soils here are high in both quartz and mica, stamping the wines with a fine minerality.

In this *federspiel* (second top in the Wachau quality league) example sourced from multiple steep terraced vineyards (a.k.a. *terrassen*) around the Wachau valley, expect ripe citrus and apricot fruit with aromas of wet wool, pepper, and spice. The palate is steely and rich, with fresh acidity and a dry, snappy finish.

get it from...

£8.34

Handford Wines
Planet of the Grapes
Imbibros
Vineyards : Sherborne
Alliance Wines

Codorníu Pinot Noir Brut Rosé NV
Penedès Spain

I've said it before, but there's something very liberating about fish and chips on the beach, toes in the sand, decent company, and a good bottle of bubbles within arm's reach. Wines with plenty of acidity and bubbles really come into their own here, working to cut through oil and batter, while simultaneously leaving your palate clean and refreshed. A little bit of salt and lemon doesn't hurt things either, although it's advisable to take it easy on the latter.

From Spanish bubbles giant Codorníu, this utterly mouth-watering Rosé Cava made from 100 per cent Pinot Noir has an attractive nose of fresh summer berries and a palate that's both lively and well-structured.

get it from...

£10.99

Majestic
Wine Warehouse

Oddbins

Thresher

Wine Rack

Codorníu UK

Kaesler
Stonehorse 2007
Barossa Valley
Australia

After a century of grape-growing and supplying fruit to some of the industry's bigger players, the historic Kaesler vineyards, which had been bought and sold a number of times, finally went it alone.

From a cracking range of wines, Stonehouse GSM is a fruit-rich, drink-now blend of Grenache (45 per cent), Shiraz (44 per cent), and Mourvèdre (11 per cent) taken from old, low-yielding Barossa vines ranging between 20 and 45 years of age. Concentrated and pure, aromas here range from sweet blackberry through to raspberry, plum, and creamy milk chocolate, while in your mouth it's lush, fruit-driven, and nicely balanced by a wash of fine tannins. Incorporated oak is of the older kind, and the wine is bottled without fining or filtration.

get it from...

£10.30

Tanners Wine Merchants

J M da Fonseca Periquita White 2008 Terras do Sado Portugal

Portugal's new wave of dry table wines has created a serious buzz on a number of fronts – particularly in the value-for-money stakes. From the stables of José Maria da Fonseca, one of Portugal's oldest and most iconic producers, Periquita is a box-fresh and mouth-watering blend of Moscatel de Setúbal (80 per cent) and Arinto (20 per cent) from the sandy soils of the Setúbal Peninsula.

Expect aromas of lime juice, orange blossom, apricot, and minerals, while in your mouth it's rich in stone-fruit intensity, with lowish acidity and a clean, dry finish. A small proportion of the Moscatel spends some time in oak, while the rest is fermented cool in stainless steel tanks.

get it from...

£6.49

Waitrose
HMWSA

Treat your wine with respect

Wine likes to be stored in a cool, dark spot away from vibration, and also safe from the threat of thirsty housemates.

Vasse Felix Semillon/ Sauvignon Blanc 2009 Margaret River Australia

For those thinking it's only the French who have all the fun blending these two varieties, think again. For many moons now Western Australian producers have been carving mouth-watering examples from the duo – this stylish and ever-consistent offering from Vasse Felix being no exception. Here, personality and charm come courtesy of Sauvignon Blanc, while the ever-reliable Semillon provides a rock-solid foundation upon which to build.

Expect a big nose full of Sicilian lemons along with piercing gooseberry and split-pea character, while the palate is fresh as a daisy and punctuated by the kind of lip-smacking acidity that makes this wine almost impossible to put down.

get it from...

£11.99

Highbury Vintners

White Vin Man

Flagship Wines

Berkmann Wine Cellars

Negociants UK

Turkey Flat
Rosé 2007
Barossa Valley
Australia

My last three-day visit to the Barossa was set against a backdrop of 37°C (99°F) heat – not the most comfortable conditions for a feeble city type like me, but a truly memorable experience nonetheless. Memorable mainly for the excessive amount of great rosé we drank in a bid to try and reduce our core temperatures, and it was this example from Turkey Flat that got me all worked up in the process.

Pretty pink, this wine has Barossa stamped all over it. Bone-dry and loaded with plenty of personality and charm, expect a nose of bright raspberry and redcurrant fruit, while in your mouth it's super-refreshing, moderately fruity, and clean as a whistle.

get it from...

£9.99

Harrods
Selfridges & Co
Noel Young Wines
Whole Foods Market
Mentzendorff

Cumulus
Climbing Merlot 2006
Orange
Australia

The Climbing and Rolling ranges from Cumulus pay homage to Orange and New South Wales's Central Ranges respectively. The Climbing wines focus on the high-altitude vineyards of Orange, where an extended growing season and free-draining, gravel-rich soils provide an excellent starting point for Merlot, among others.

Deep purple, this is plush and fruit-rich Merlot, with oodles of intensity and flavour. Expect a nose of sweet black fruits, bitter dark chocolate, and polished leather. The palate is sweet, rich, and nicely framed by fine, drying tannins.

get it from...

£9.99

Majestic Wine Warehouse
mollybrownswinelist.co.uk

Boekenhoutskloof
The Wolftrap Rosé 2008
Franschhoek
South Africa

Regular readers of this guide will know that I've long been a fan of Marc Kent, the brains behind the winemaking controls at Boekenhoutskloof. Both Kent's flagship Syrah and wines from the much-loved Porcupine Ridge range have graced the pages of previous editions, and remain some of my favourite South African wines.

Kent's bargain basement Wolftrap range, which includes one of the rosés of the summer, doesn't disappoint either. Assembled from Syrah (61 per cent), Cinsault (27 per cent), and Grenache Noir (12 per cent), this is a lively, fresh, and dry style of rosé where restrained fruit and mouth-watering acidity make it as good with food as without.

get it from...

£6.99

Oddbins
Cape Wine & Food
New Generation Wines

Donnafugata
Anthìlia 2008
Sicily
Italy

A sure-fire contender for feel-good hit of the summer, Anthìlia is a clean and refreshing, equal-parts mix of local Sicilian varieties Ansonica (a.k.a. Inzolia) and Catarratto from Sicilian stars Donnafugata. Production is short and sharp, with fermentation cool and quick, taking place in stainless steel prior to filtering and bottling.

Pale straw to look at, the nose shows plenty of bright grapefruit-citrus fruit, alongside aromas of green herbs and minerals, and with zero oak influence. The palate is tight, clean, and dry with stunning intensity of ripe stone fruit – all of which is framed with an acidity so fresh it almost hurts.

get it from...

£8.99

Majestic
Wine Warehouse

Liberty Wines

Beware of gimmicks

The world of wine accessories is full of them, including vacuum-style wine pumps. While sucking excess oxygen out of a bottle, most also have a nasty habit of taking aroma molecules with them, leaving your wine "stripped" of all those lovely smells.

Dr Loosen
Graacher Himmelreich
Riesling Kabinett 2007
Mosel
Germany

The precariously steep vineyards surrounding the village of Graach lie on the right bank of the Mosel and form part of the 6km (4-mile) stretch that encompasses the villages of Bernkastel, Graach, and Wehlen. Specifically, the 87-hectare Himmelreich vineyard is planted exclusively to Riesling and is situated on a bed of clay and blue slate. So, as you can probably imagine, Ernie Loosen's version is worth walking over hot coals for.

Bursting bright green/gold to look at, this has one of the prettiest noses I've smelt in a long time, with mandarin, lime, and fresh flowers all vying for attention. The palate is pure, mineral, and intensely flavoured – flavour that resonates long after the wine has left your mouth.

get it from...

£14.49

Sainsbury's
ABS Wine Agencies

Telmo Rodríguez
Basa Blanco 2008
Rueda
Spain

Five years after we named this wine Bargain of the Year it's back, and for all the same reasons. The Telmo Rodríguez stable knows how to do style and value better than most, and this box-fresh blend of Verdejo, Viura, and Sauvignon Blanc will have you scratching your head in amazement at how on earth it continues to charge such reasonable prices for such knockout wines.

Basa – or base as it translates – is the keenly priced white star of the Rodríguez stable, and it's a great place to start. Expect aromas of gooseberry, lemon, and fresh spring peas to hit you with in-your-face intensity. The palate is zippy, clean as a whistle and packed with restrained passion-fruit/lemony flavour.

get it from...

£7.29

Adnams Cellar & Kitchen

Bouchard Père & Fils Fleurie 2007
Beaujolais France

The Bouchard star has been on the rise ever since being purchased by Henriot in 1995. No expense has been spared in pursuit of excellence, and the last few vintages have put it among Burgundy's finest names. Beyond the bounds of the Cote d'Or they also make some pretty handy examples of Beaujolais.

Made from 100 per cent Gamay and taken from the Beaujolais *cru* of Fleurie, this example is packed with bright and bouncy red summer fruit, fresh flowers, and zero oak influence. And, if patience happens to be one of your virtues, it will happily endure a little time in an ice bucket prior to being guzzled.

get it from...

£9.99

Waitrose

J E Fells & Sons

Ravenswood Vintners Blend Zinfandel 2005 Multi-district blend California

While the Ravenswood catch phrase is "no wimpy wines", this delicious drink-now red is a little more metro-sexual than they might like you to think – and I'm good with that! For starters, there's far less oak incorporated into this wine than those a couple of pegs up the Ravenswood pecking order.

Although a straight-up snapshot of young Zinfandel from multiple sources, the fruit is nowhere near as intense as that found in the Ravenswood single-vineyard wines. Aromas range from pure dark cherry to sweet blood plum, while in your mouth it's plush, simple, and soft, which, given the selling price, equates to superb everyday drinking.

get it from...

£7.69

Waitrose
Somerfield

Care about what you drink? Care about what you drink from

Decent glasses needn't cost you a fortune, but they will make a huge difference to the taste of your wine. Store them in a well-ventilated place – not a cardboard box – and hand-wash them in warm, soapy water rather than the dishwasher.

Charles Joguet
Les Petites Roches
Chinon 2007
Loire
France

Charles Joguet redefined how things were done in Chinon. In the vineyard the Cabernet Franc master reduced yields, harvested by hand, and picked only into small crates in a bid to protect and preserve the fruit, while in the winery he fermented in stainless steel rather than concrete, and was a big advocate of site-driven wines rather than blends.

One of the more everyday Joguet wines, Les Petites Roches is a fresh and lively example of Cabernet Franc taken from 30- to 40-year-old vines in the gravelly north west of Chinon. Bright raspberry and redcurrant fruit dominate alongside aromas of smoke and earth. The palate is plump, mineral, and fine, with dry, chalky tannins and a clean, balanced finish.

get it from...

£9.45

Waitrose
Charles Sydney

d'Arenberg
The Noble Wrinkled
Riesling 2008
McLaren Vale
Australia

d'Arenberg has been growing grapes in McLaren Vale for near enough 100 years. For many moons it was a supplier of grapes to South Australia's bigger players, but by the late 1920s it had decided to go it alone, turning at least some of its attention to making wine too. Today, as then, vineyards are dry-farmed, minimal sprays are used, and everything that can be done by hand is. Winemaking is handled by Chester Osborn, the fourth generation member of the d'Arenberg clan.

The Noble Wrinkled Riesling takes its name from the shrivelling effect that the botrytis fungus has on grape skins. Expect a nose overflowing with ripe stone fruit, sweet orange marmalade, and spice, while the palate is bright and full but not cloying, with a long, crisp finish.

get it from...

£10.99 (37.5 cl)

Unwined Ltd
Corks & Cases
Grapeland Ltd
Bibendum Wine

Green Point
Brut NV
Multi-district blend
Australia

Green Point is located in the postcard-perfect Yarra Valley, about two cappuccino's drive east of Melbourne. It was established by Moët & Chandon in 1986 with a view to producing top-end New World sparkling wine, made in the traditional style. This non-vintage brut was sourced from a range of cool-climate regions around Australia including the Yarra Valley, the Strathbogie Ranges, the King and Buffalo Valleys, Coonawarra, and Tasmania.

Calling on the Champagne trio of Chardonnay, Pinot Noir, and Pinot Meunier, expect restrained aromas of citrus/stone fruit, toast, and honey, while in your mouth it's full and rich, with plenty of small, bright bubbles and a long, dry finish.

get it from...

£12.99

Oddbins

Majestic
Wine Warehouse

Harvey Nichols

LVMH

J L Wolf
Wachenheimer
Riesling 2007
Pfalz
Germany

Ernie Loosen, our esteemed Producer of the Year, is a busy man. Multiple collaborations aside, he also runs two successful domaines – Dr Loosen in the Mosel and J L Wolf in the Pfalz. While the J L Wolf history extends back over 200 years, it's the last ten from which the significant advances have come.

Having taken control of the estate in 1996, Loosen quickly set about training his focus on the J L Wolf vineyards. The results are amazing. From the village vineyard series, the Wachenheimer Riesling is one of those classic wines that walks the tightrope between sweetness and acidity with ease. Combining smells of jasmine, mandarin, spice, and lime, with a racy palate that pulls up just this side of dry.

get it from...
£10.95

Great Western Wine
ABS Wine Agencies

Invest in a decent corkscrew

I know it sounds ridiculous, but it will pay for itself. I have ruined more great bottles of wine than I care to remember by using cheap corkscrews trying to open them. Look for something with an easy action, something that feels strong, and if you can, an opener with a Teflon-coated screw.

Reichsrat von Buhl Riesling Trocken 2008 Pfalz Germany

RIESLING
TROCKEN

Reichsrat von Buhl has been a family affair for the past 150 years, having originally been transferred by the von Buhl estate to family friend George Enoch von und zu Guttenberg in the early 1920s. Since that time the estate has endured both the highs and lows of the wine world, and has more recently flourished thanks to a couple of much-needed capital injections. Wines here are big on fruit and comfortably straddle the fence between modern and traditional.

This *trocken* or "dry" Riesling is a cracker. Although really only "dry" by German standards, expect aromas of jasmine, musk, lemon rind, and minerals, while the palate is crisp and pure, with cleansing acidity and an off-dry finish.

get it from...

£8.95

Harrods

Abbey Wines

Jascots Wine Merchants

Wildflower Wines

World Wine Agencies (Bath) Ltd

Peter Lehmann Wigan Eden Valley Riesling 2004
Eden Valley
Australia

Andrew Wigan, the man behind the winemaking controls at Peter Lehmann, is crazy about Riesling. Having made every Riesling under the Peter Lehmann label since its conception in 1979, this wine pays homage to Wigan's commitment to the variety, and to the belief that Eden Valley Riesling is among the finest of its kind in Australia.

The nose is explosive and bright with pure essence of lime, mandarin, fresh summer flowers, and spice, while once inside your mouth this wine just unleashes lime-juice intensity so pure, so long, and so well balanced that it'll blow your mind. Laser-like acidity should be enough to ensure it remains with us for many moons to come.

get it from...

£11.99

Enotria Winecellars
Peter Lehmann UK

Concha y Toro Terrunyo Sauvignon Blanc 2008 Casablanca Chile

Terrunyo – the Spanish word for the French word *terroir* that has no straightforward English translation. Confused? Monty Python-like as it might sound, a combination of gravelly soils coupled with the cooling breezes of the Pacific Ocean make the area of Casablanca ideal for the production of A-grade Sauvignon Blanc. Apart from just the faintest hint of green in the glass, any trace of colour is virtually nonexistent.

The nose is a different story altogether, with intense smells of passion-fruit, gooseberry, and blackcurrant alongside those of fresh cut grass and spring peas. The palate is fruity, fresh, clean, crisp, and mineral.

get it from...

£9.99

The Wine Society

Corks Out

Corkscrew Wines

Concha y Toro UK

Wente Morning Fog Chardonnay 2008 Livermore Valley California

Sun-loving Chardonnay has long been a happy resident of California. But where a lot of Californian Chardonnay has historically been overenthusiastically super-sized with both oak and fruit, this example from the cool of the San Francisco Bay area manages to effortlessly knit both, while still retaining serious charm and elegance.

From its compact, lemony nose, which displays subtle aromas of apple, pear, sweet spice, hazelnut, and minerals, to its intense and finely structured palate, this is a great illustration of just how good New World Chardonnay can be.

get it from...

£7.99

Waitrose

Thresher

Stevens Garnier

Co-op Fairtrade Argentine Organic Malbec Reserve 2008
Famatina Valley Argentina

Located in the Famatina Valley, La Riojana is the largest cooperative in Argentina and received Fairtrade accreditation in 2006. Because the co-op acts on behalf of a number of different communities, they have decided that, in the short term, funds raised will be directed towards improving local water supplies.

With all the style and substance of many pricier New World wines, expect masses of dark, sun-drenched fruit on the nose, coupled with aromas of dried spice and tobacco. It's a case of dense, dark, and chewy on the palate too, with a wave of ripe dark fruit, spicy new oak, and a wash of dry, grippy tannins.

get it from...

£6.49

The Co-op

Telmo Rodríguez
Viña 105 2008
Cigales
Spain

High up in Spain's central-northwestern corner, straddling the borders of Ribera del Duero and Rueda, is the increasingly fashionable region of Cigales. Red variety Tempranillo is the local star, producing fresh, fruit-driven wines with bright acidity and dry, grippy tannins.

In the case of this example, great old-vine fruit coupled with the Midas touch of winemaker Telmo Rodríguez – one of my favourite Spanish winemakers – has produced a wine layered with cassis, cherry, smoke, and spice. There is little, if any, evidence of oak, making this a delicious drink-now proposition.

get it from...

£7.50

Adnams Cellar & Kitchen

Be wary of "special offers"

From experience, "special offers" are rarely all that special. If you really want to find the bargains on the supermarket wine shelf, do a bit of research and seek out the weird and wonderful: new varieties, styles, regions, and countries that you have never heard of. More often than not, that's where the real value lies.

Delta Vineyard Pinot Noir 2008 Marlborough New Zealand

The combination of Kiwi winemaker Matt Thomson and Canadian-born MW David Gleave is a formidable one. Together they are responsible for Delta – a Marlborough-based venture committed to producing top-drawer New World Pinot Noir. Site selection was paramount, and while elsewhere in New Zealand Martinborough might boast the oldest vines in the country, and Central Otago a dreamy mix of clones, examples like this show that Marlborough can comfortably mix it with the best of them.

Showing real varietal character and charm, expect a generous nose of sour-cherry and raspberry fruit, while silky texture, fine-grained tannin, and great length of flavour define a sleek and stylish mouthful of wine.

get it from...

£12.99

The Wine Society

Wimbledon Wine Cellar

Luvians Bottleshop

The New Zealand House of Wine

Liberty Wines

25 wines for indulging

Welcome to the chapter where we throw caution to the wind and bravely show the budget the door. First and foremost, know that the wines that appear over the coming pages are not here because of what they cost but rather what they're worth. Know that a huge investment of love, blood, sweat, and tears is more often than not required to produce these wines – some of which are already established benchmarks, while others are modern classics in the making. Finally, remember that with wine you generally get what you pay for, and so in the case of the following 25 bottles, mega attention to detail, microscopic productions, and well-earned reputations count for everything.

Splurge

Clonakilla O'Riada Shiraz 2007 Canberra District Australia

With only a minute amount of his flagship Shiraz/Viognier being made in 2007, the devastating frosts of that year forced Tim Kirk to look further afield. He produced a new wine from selected parcels of fruit taken from around the Murrumbateman area near Canberra. And the result, weighing in at much less than his brilliant and much sought-after Shiraz/Viognier, is the delicious and more affordable O'Riada Shiraz.

Co-fermented with two per cent Viognier, prepare yourself for explosive aromatics that include dark cherry, blood plum, pepper, tobacco, and five-spice. The palate is pure and focused, with sweet, plummy fruit taking charge and gentle, drying tannins to finish.

get it from...

£26.99

Noel Young Wines
Philglas & Swiggot
Villeneuve Wines
Liberty Wines

Bodegas Hidalgo La Gitana Amontillado Napoleon Jerez Spain

While Hidalgo's knockout popular La Gitana Manzanilla is no stranger to the pages of this guide, it's the dry Napoleon amontillado from the premium range that's really grabbed my attention this year. And I can't believe that it's escaped my attention until now!

Dry, nutty, and complex, this is sherry for serving at room temperature, sherry for drinking with things like smoked fish and salty cured meats, sherry for savouring. A copper colour leads to a dry, nutty nose charged with aromas of cedar, smoke, and spice, while in your mouth it's bright and citrus-like, before descending into a long, drying, nutty finish.

get it from...

£12.99

Majestic
Wine Warehouse

Noel Young Wines

Brindisa Wholesale

Fenwick

Mentzendorff

Hess
Monterey
Chardonnay 2007
Monterey
California

After a long-overdue makeover, Chardonnay is back. Gone is the once-golden appearance, the flabby fruit, the charry oak, and the everything-but-the-kitchen-sink approach that used to turn so many of us away in droves. Chardonnay c.2010, it would seem, has finally learned how to look good naked. Taken from the cool Shirtail vineyard in Monterey, this example from Californian producer Hess is a great illustration of Chardonnay's new breed.

Aromatics here range from grapefruit to nectarine, while the palate shows soft citrus fruit, mineral texture, and terrific length of flavour.

get it from...

£15.50

Majestic
Wine Warehouse

Pure Wines

The Vine Shop

The Secret Cellar

Latitude Wine &
Liquor Merchant

Enotria Winecellars

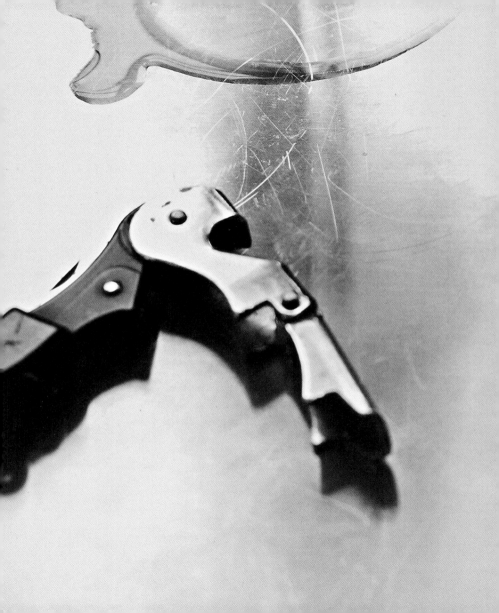

Pegasus Bay Sauvignon Blanc/ Semillon 2007 Canterbury New Zealand

In the beautiful Waipara valley outside Christchurch, the Donaldson family craft some of New Zealand's finest white wines. Besides great examples of Chardonnay and Riesling, they also make one of the slickest blends of Sauvignon Blanc and Semillon I have ever had the good fortune of tasting.

Textured and refined, this is a breathtaking blend where an extended period on lees and the judicious use of oak have paid off big time. Expect a complex nose of white peach, pear, and passion-fruit, while broad stone-fruit flavour is carried in the mouth by creamy texture and framed by focused acidity and terrific length. Seamless, long, drinking beautifully now, yet built to last.

get it from...

£16.00

Cambridge Wine Merchants

Handford Wines

The New Zealand House of Wine

Fine Wines of New Zealand

Caviste

New Generation Wines

Millton Te Arai Chenin Blanc 2007 Gisborne New Zealand

James and Annie Millton established the Millton Vineyard in Gisborne in 1984, having returned from working in the vineyards of Europe. Champions of the biodynamic movement, the Milltons produce a range of wines via sound ecological practices that ensure the balance and health of their vineyards and all things within. The Te Arai vineyards lie just 5km (3 miles) from the sea and provide a happy hunting ground for Chenin Blanc, with mist from the Te Arai waterways encouraging some botrytis activity.

Expect to find crème brûlée, cashew, grapefruit, nectarine, and pork rind on the nose, while in your mouth it's rich and intense with mineral texture and jawdropping length of flavour.

get it from...

£12.50

Budgens
As Nature Intended
Berits & Brown
Hammerton Store
Vintage Roots

Keep it interesting

It's easy to fall into a wine rut, so make it your business to try new things whenever you get the chance. Sommeliers, wine waiters, and those behind the counter of your local are not out to get you! Put your faith in them and let them pick something for you.

Bründlmayer Grüner Veltliner Kamptaler Terrassen 2008 Kamptal Austria

The Bründlmayer estate employs sound ecological practices with a definite nod to organic and biodynamic farming. No chemical fertilizers, herbicides, pesticides, or fungicides are used in the vineyards, and when old vines are removed, the soil is given a minimum of five years to regenerate. This is rich and racy Grüner from one of Austria's largest fine wine-growing area, the Kamptal, carrying aromas and flavours of white peach, wet wool, and spice.

With Riesling occupying the best of the higher sites within the area, the lower-altitude, clay-rich soils closer to the Danube River provide the perfect spot for the cultivation of Grüner Veltliner. A stunning illustration of just how good this estate is.

get it from...

£12.49

Tanners Wine Merchants

WoodWinters Wines & Whiskies

Raeburn Fine Wines

Amps Fine Wines

Richards Walford

Zind-Humbrecht
Zind 2006
Alsace
France

Olivier Humbrecht MW is both a fierce stickler for detail and a true champion of the biodynamic movement. His wines are produced via an enormous amount of effort, which includes high-density planting, everything that can be done by hand being done by hand, alcoholic fermentation of all wines in oak, and all vineyard tasks organized and carried out in line with the various phases of the moon.

The attention to detail is as astonishing as the wines. The entry-level Zind is a medium-bodied, off-dry, drink-now blend of Chardonnay and Auxerrois Blanc produced in the house style, and loaded with ripe stone and tropical fruit character.

get it from...

£14.99

Waitrose

First Drop Mother's Milk Shiraz 2004 Barossa Valley Australia

Anyone who believes that Australian wine has become drab/bland/mediocre/one-dimensional need look no further than the second instalment of Mother's Milk from the First Drop team. Anything but ordinary, this is the Barossa New School at its finest, forging deliciously drinkable and affordable wines that you don't need a knife and fork for.

Cool, dark fruit coupled with a judicious use of oak (15 months in 95 per cent old French oak hogsheads with just a smidge of new American making up the numbers) make this drink-now wine well worth the hunt – although with little more than 2,000 cases made, you'd be wise to get hunting sooner rather than later.

get it from...

£15.99

Oz Wines

Chapel Down Brut NV
Kent England

Forty-seven miles from London (a very leisurely Sunday's drive) is Tenterden, home to Chapel Down – England's largest producer of high-quality sparkling wine. Yet it wasn't so long ago that simply finding a decent English sparkling wine was a tough assignment. Now, thanks to greater expertise, better technology, and a deeper understanding of both climate and site, English bubbles have never looked better.

Following production methods used in Champagne, this drink-now blend of Rivaner, Reichensteiner, and Pinot Noir is rich with smells of green apples and lemon sherbet, while in your mouth a charge of tiny bubbles and great flavour round things off nicely. If you've never been to a vineyard, let alone an English one, now would be the time.

get it from...

£16.99

Waitrose
Booths
Wine Rack
Selfridges & Co
English Wines Group

Kangarilla Road Primitivo 2007 Fleurieu Australia

Zinfandel, Primitivo – call it what you will, but the best examples of this variety will almost always display masses of dark, sun-drenched fruit, liquorice, and leather on the nose, while a mouthful will often reveal a lush, inky wave of ripe dark fruit, spicy new oak, and a wash of dry, grippy tannins.

As a result, big wines such as this example from Kangarilla Road need big food to match. Carnivores should seek out the best hamburger recipe they can find and, together with the help of a couple of rashers of smoked streaky bacon, a slice of mature Cheddar, a fried egg, lettuce, tomato, beetroot, onion, spicy relish, and a sourdough bun – toasted only on the inside – they'll be joining the dots to create Zinfandel magic.

get it from...

£11.99

Villeneuve Wines

Cambridge Wine Merchants

Peckham & Rye

Indage (UK) Ltd

Rediscover your sweet tooth

Don't turn your nose up at sweet wines.
Sweet wines rarely get the kudos they
deserve and more often than not they will
represent some of the greatest value on
a wine list. Problem is that by the time we
get to them we've usually had enough.
Next time, save some room.

Tamar Ridge Kayena Vineyard Pinot Noir 2006 Tamar Valley Tasmania

Pinot Noir is incredibly versatile with food. From raw tuna, to trout, to mushrooms, truffles, chicken, lamb, rabbit, hare, quail, squab, teal, grouse, pheasant, pigeon, partridge, and duck – the possibilities for great matches with Pinot Noir are seemingly endless. You'll even find an amazing Pinot partner in salmon. It's an almost spiritual relationship. At best, both are rich, decadent, and have terrific intensity of flavour and delicate textures. One is naturally high in fat, while the other loves nothing more than gently slicing through it.

As Tasmanian Pinot Noir goes from strength to strength, this fine example from Tamar Valley's Kayena Vineyard in West Tamar is plush, finely tuned, and an ideal salmon partner.

get it from...

£14.99

Noel Young Wines
Averys Wine Merchants
Novum
ABS Wine Agencies

Roederer Estate Quartet Brut NV Anderson Valley USA

Quartet is the first, and much underrated, sparkling wine produced in the USA by the iconic Champagne house of Louis Roederer. Okay, so Cristal it's not, but blended from four distinct vineyards of varying soil type and altitude, this is a very real essay in style and value, where Chardonnay – some of which has spent a bit of time in oak – takes the lead.

Expect to find smells and flavours of fresh bread, marzipan, and rich citrus marmalade, while in the mouth it's long, fine, and packed with all the TLC you'd expect from one of Champagne's greatest names.

get it from...

£23.50

Waitrose

Majestic
Wine Warehouse

Quaff Fine Wine Merchant

Four Walls
Wine Company

Maison Marques
& Domaines

Henschke
Tilly's Vineyard 2007
South Australia
Australia

Henschke is renowned the world over as a classy producer, but it's not only its top Hill of Grace red, one of Australia's most revered wines, that offers an indulgent experience. At the other end of the spectrum is Tilly's Vineyard, a beautifully elegant white that represents seriously good value.

Lovingly assembled from Semillon (57 per cent), Sauvignon Blanc (24 per cent), and Chardonnay (19 per cent), and using fruit drawn from both the Barossa Valley and the Adelaide Hills, expect smells of lemon rind, elderflower, and green herbs, while in the mouth it's vibrant, zippy, and dry. Prior to bottling, a fraction of the wine spends nine months on lees in new French oak, giving the wine weight and texture, while keeping the use of oak to a minimum.

get it from...

£12.99

Lay & Wheeler
Wheeler Cellars
Noel Young Wines
Wine in Cornwall
Enotria Winecellars

Drink more fortified wine

Port, sherry, liqueur Muscat, and Tokay – these are the endangered species of the wine world. They are also some of the most amazing wines produced in the world, yet because of their higher alcohol content and our taste for drier wines, they are also some of the most unpopular. Please support them before they disappear from our shelves forever.

Cosme Palacio
y Hermanos
Rioja Reserva 2004
Rioja
Spain

Comfort wine. It's like your mum's roast, like a familiar face waiting to greet you at the airport, like the smell of fresh coffee. That's how Cosme Palacio Rioja Reserva makes me feel. Comfortable. This is straight-up, good old-fashioned Rioja, with no muscle and nothing artificial – just great fruit and three years of ageing, some of which took place in oak.

Brick/garnet to look at, the nose is spiced cherry and dried fruits together with fresh rolling tobacco and sweet spice smells. The palate falls toward the lighter side of medium bodied and provides a brilliant snapshot of this world-famous region.

get it from...

£12.99

Tesco
Sainsbury's
Asda
Waitrose
J E Fells & Sons

Punt Road
Pinot Gris 2008
Yarra Valley
Australia

Punt Road, one of the worst streets in Melbourne, is a major arterial road connecting the northern suburbs with those in the south. If you're unlucky enough to be on Punt Road, then you're bound to be going slowly, if at all. Thankfully, the other Punt Road – one of the finest wine producers in the Yarra Valley – is far more reliable.

My current fave from the range is the knockout Pinot Gris, a beautifully crafted wine that is hand-harvested, whole-bunch pressed, and fermented cool with some time in oak. Soft stone fruits such as pears and peaches lead the charge on the nose, while the palate is broad, long, and nicely textured.

get it from...

£13.99

Noel Young Wines
Four Walls Wine Company
City Beverage Company
The House of Menzies
PLB Group Ltd

Sánchez Romate
Cardenal Cisneros
Pedro Ximénez NV
Jerez
Spain

Wow. As a self-confessed sherry freak, I would be the first to admit that I love PX for its over-the-top liquid Christmas cake aromatics, for its plush, velvety mouth-feel, and for its long-as-you-like finish that just seems to go on forever. But this is ridiculous. This takes the good old PX experience to a new level.

Take a seat and brace yourself for a nose full of dried raisin fruit, molasses, treacle, Middle Eastern spices, and freshly ground coffee. In the mouth it borders on pouring cream consistency and comes fully loaded with sweet raisined fruit and cloying intensity. Dried-raisin fruit coupled with aromas of cinnamon, nutmeg, and clove lead to a mouthful of sweet, rich, and cloying fruit, with wave after wave of intensity.

get it from...

£21.99

Selfridges & Co
Philglas & Swiggot
Great Western Wine
Les Caves de Pyrene
Eaux de Vie

Lustau
Emelín Moscatel
Solera Reserve NV
Jerez
Spain

One of two sweet Moscatels made by Lustau and a step back from the glorious San Emilio PX, Emilín Moscatel is surprisingly light, but still comes packing plenty of personality.

For starters, it's much paler to look at, with a solid, deep copper colour extending right toward the outer rim of your glass. The nose is lighter too. Bright and lifted aromas of dried raisins, sweet spice, and oak – of which this wine has seen its share – are all there. The palate is spirity and fresh with plenty of raisiny fruit flavour, yet minus the cloy factor. Be warned: it's a dangerously easy wine to drink and the finish is sweet, oaky, and long.

get it from...

£16.30 (37.5 cl)

Fortnum & Mason
Quaff Fine Wine Merchant
Caviste
Corks Out
Fields, Morris, & Verdin

Avoid the second-cheapest bottle

The second-cheapest bottle on the wine list is never the best value – every wine buyer on the planet knows that trick. Invest your trust in the sommelier, the wine waiter, or the waiting staff. Give them some parameters on price and style etc., and then let them recommend something for you.

Cuvaison Chardonnay Carneros 2007 Napa Valley California

Sun-loving Chardonnay has long been a happy resident of California. But where a lot of Californian Chardonnay has historically been overenthusiastically super-sized with both oak and fruit, this example from the cool of Carneros manages to effortlessly knit both, while still retaining serious charm and elegance.

From its compact, lemony nose that includes subtle smells of apple, pear, sweet spice, hazelnut, and minerals, to its intense and finely structured palate, this is a great illustration of just how good New World Chardonnay can be. Having spent eight months in French oak, a third of which is new, the wine is beautifully knitted together.

get it from...

£19.20

Tanners Wine Merchants

Noel Young Wines

Field & Fawcett Wine Merchants & Delicatessen

Uncorked Wine Merchants

Thorman Hunt & Co Ltd

Domaine Tempier
Bandol Rosé 2008
Provence
France

There's only a couple of wines whose impending annual arrival manages to get my heart racing. Tempier Rosé is one of them. Located on France's south coast halfway between Marseille and Toulon, and brought to the wine-loving world's attention by engaging, enterprising Californian wine merchant Kermit Lynch, (he of the famed *Adventures on the Wine Route*) Tempier is renowned for its five terroir-driven *cuvées* of old-vine Mourvèdre, and for its rosé, which boasts a serious cult-like following.

Produced from a mix of Mourvèdre, Grenache, and Cinsault, and with only a tiny amount of time in contact with the skins, the result is a clean, fruit-fresh, dry, and grippy rosé that will have you hooked and on the hunt in no time at all.

get it from...

£19.99

A&B Vintners
Richards Walford

Cloudy Bay Pelorus NV Marlborough New Zealand

Pelorus is the sleek and stylish sparkling wine from the stables of iconic New Zealand producer Cloudy Bay. Playing second fiddle to the flashier vintage model, this non-vintage blend incorporating Chardonnay and Pinot Noir punches well above its weight.

Expect a compact and clean nose of tart green apples, citrus, toasted brioche, and spice thanks to extended time spent on the lees, while in your mouth there's terrific intensity of ripe lemony fruit, plenty of little bubbles, and a long, balanced finish.

get it from...

£14.99

Waitrose

Majestic
Wine Warehouse

Harvey Nichols

Selfridges & Co

LVMH

Castellare di Castellina Chianti Classico 2007
Tuscany
Italy

Castellare's beautiful and often underrated Chianti Classico is certainly one of the region's smartest buys. And while many of the area's bigger names become more expensive and more concentrated by the minute, Castellare seems to maintain its cool. Straddling the boundaries between new and old, this stylish and accessible blend of Sangiovese, with a 15 per cent splash of local grapes Canaiolo and Colorino, and its annually changing image of endangered birds, effortlessly ticks all the right boxes.

Right from the word go this is unmistakably stylish Sangiovese, sporting a nose full of morello cherry, leather, and tobacco, while in your mouth it's plush, mineral-textured, and framed by trademark fine, chalky tannins, finishing clean and dry.

get it from...

£15.50

Handford Wines

Borough Wines

A Moveable Feast Ltd

Huntsworth Wine Co Ltd

FortyFive10°

S C Pannell
Pronto Bianco 2008
Adelaide Hills
Australia

The cold, rough waters of the Atlantic skirting Spain's northwest are home to a staggering range of sealife that includes everything from oysters, cockles, clams, and scallops to whitebait, prawns, mackerel, eel, and lobster. In short, it's seafood heaven and there's an abundance of great wine matches to be had here too. The best-suited wines tend to be those with some weight and texture.

Steve Pannell's Pronto Bianco – a wine from about as far away from Spain's northwest corner as you could possibly get – is a confident blend of Sauvignon Blanc, Riesling, and Pinot Gris that has delicious aromatics, great intensity of flavour, nice weight and texture, and a clean, dry finish.

get it from...

£12.99

Noel Young Wines

Philglas & Swiggot

Cornelius Beer & Wine

Liberty Wines

Speak up!

If you're not happy with your wine,
tell the sommelier/wine waiter.
That said, you will really only have
grounds to return the wine if it's
corked or oxidized. If you simply
don't like it, chances are you'll be
stuck with it.

André Clouet
Silver Brut NV
Champagne
France

Small-scale and grower Champagnes remain all the rage in 2010, and this highly gluggable wine from André Clouet is right up the top of my favourites list. This delicious estate-bottled, non-vintage blend is 100 per cent Pinot Noir and draws on fruit from the *grand cru* Champagne village of Bouzy.

Expect aromas of toast, citrus, honey, and spice coupled with masses of fine, persistent bubbles, great length of flavour, and a long, tight finish. Thirty months on the lees prior to disgorgement helps to make this wine one of the best-value examples of *blanc de noirs* Champagne on the market.

get it from...

£22.95

Tanners Wine Merchants

Ayala
Brut Nature
Zéro Dosage NV
Champagne
France

The wines of Ayala have improved out of sight ever since Bollinger purchased the property in late 2005. Yet, in stark contrast to Bollinger, Ayala's style relies on being lighter and fresher, making it a brilliant pre-dinner option. The mouth-watering Brut Zéro Dosage – reference to the fact that this wine was bottled without the addition of any sweetened base wine *(dosage)* – is the ultimate aperitif, incorporating a ruthless selection process and utilizing fruit from selected *grand* and *premier cru* vineyards.

With Pinot Noir taking the leading role, expect restrained citrus and stone fruit, toast, and honey. Meanwhile, the palate is full and rich, with plenty of bright bubbles and a long, dry finish.

get it from...
£26.00

Quintessentially Wine
drinksdirect.co.uk
Mentzendorff

Pol Roger
1999
Champagne
France

Having already scooped the prize for the most under-appreciated, non-vintage fizz on the market, Pol Roger is set for a repeat performance with its knockout vintage version. Words struggle to describe just how consistently good this wine is, and much like its stable mate, it's simply an essay in both style and value.

Aromas of Pinot Noir fruit and fresh toasted brioche set you up for a mouthful of rich stone and citrus fruit that's creamy and direct, with firm acidity and incredible length of flavour – a genuine jawdropper from one of Champagne's greatest houses.

get it from...

£47.99

Majestic
Wine Warehouse

Berry Bros & Rudd

The Wine Society

Jeroboams & Laytons

Pol Roger UK

Stockists

UK

A&B Vintners
www.abvintners.co.uk
01892 724977

Abbey Wines
01896 823224

ABS (Awin Barratt Siegel)
Wine Agencies
www.abswineagencies.co.uk
01780 755810

Adnams Cellar & Kitchen
cellarandkitchen.adnams.co.uk
01502 727222

Alliance Wines
www.alliancewine.co.uk
01505 506060

A Moveable Feast Ltd
www.amfwine.com
07870 384 490

Amps Fine Wines
www.ampsfinewines.co.uk
01832 273502

Asda
www.asda.co.uk

As Nature Intended
www.asnatureintended.uk.com
020 8840 4856

Australian Vintage Ltd
www.australianvintage.com.au

Australian Wines Online
www.australianwinesonline.co.uk
01772 422996

Averys Wine Merchants
www.averys.com
0845 8630995

Bacchanalia
01223 315034

Bentalls
www.bentalls.co.uk

Berits & Brown
www.beritsandbrown.com

Berkmann Wine Cellars
www.berkmann.co.uk
020 7609 4711

Berry Bros & Rudd
www.bbr.com
0870 900 4300

Bibendum Wine
www.bibendum-wine.co.uk
020 7722 5577

Booths
www.booths-supermarkets.co.uk
01772 693800

Borough Wines
www.boroughwines.co.uk
0870 2418890

Brindisa Wholesale
www.brindisa.com
020 8772 1600

The Bristol Wine Company
www.thebristolwinecompany.co.uk
0117 373 0288

Brown Brothers Europe
www.brownbrothers.com.au
01628 776446

Brown-Forman UK
www.brown-forman.com

Budgens
www.budgens.co.uk
0800 2980758

Cambridge Wine Cellar
www.cambridgewinewarehouse.co.uk
01954 212112

Cambridge Wine Merchants
www.cambridgewine.com
01223 568991

Cape Wine & Food
www.capewineandfood.com
01784 451860

Caviste
www.caviste.co.uk
01256 770397

Charles Sydney
(+33) 247814403

Cheers Bottle Shop
01271 816160

City Beverage Company
www.citybeverage.co.uk
020 7729 2111

Codorníu UK
01892 500250

Concha y Toro UK
www.conchaytoro.com
01865 338013

Constellation
www.cbrands.eu.com
01483 690000

The Co-operative Group
www.co-operative.coop/food
0800 0686727

Corks & Cases
www.corksandcases.com
01765 688810

Corks Out
www.corksout.com
01925 267 700

Corkscrew Wines
01328 543033

Cornelius Beer & Wine
0131 652 2405

Cotswold Vintners
01454 325124

Daniel Lambert Wines Ltd
01656 661010

D Byrne & Co
www.dbyrne-finewines.co.uk
01200 423152

DeFINE Food & Wine
www.definefoodandwine.com
01606 882101

Dillons Wine Stores
01227 700236

The Dorset Wine Company
www.dorsetwine.co.uk
01305 266734

Drinksdirect.co.uk
www.drinksdirect.co.uk

Ehrmanns
www.ehrmannswines.co.uk
020 7418 1800

English Wines Group
www.englishwinesgroup.co.uk
01580 763033

Enotria Winecellars
www.enotria.co.uk
020 8961 5161

Fenwick
www.fenwick.co.uk

Field & Fawcett Wine
Merchants & Delicatessen
www.fieldandfawcett.co.uk
01904 489073

Fields, Morris, & Verdin
www.fmvwines.com
020 7921 5300

Fine Wines of New Zealand
www.fwnz.co.uk
020 7482 0093

Flagship Wines
www.flagshipwines.co.uk
01727 865309

Flint Wines
www.flintwines.com
020 7582 2210

Fortnum & Mason
www.fortnumandmason.com
020 7734 8040

FortyFive10°
www.fortyfive10.eu
07932 054376

Fosters EMEA
www.fosters.com.au

Four Walls Wine Company
www.fourwallswine.com
01243 535353

Free Run Juice
www.freerunjuice.co.uk
01872 510037

Fresh & Wild
020 7229 1063

Gauntleys of Nottingham
www.gauntley-wine.co.uk
0115 911 0555

Giles de Maré
www.demare.org.uk
01985 844695

Grapeland Ltd
www.grapeland.uk.com
01923 284436

The Great Grog Company
www.greatgrog.co.uk
0131 662 4777

Great Western Wine
www.greatwesternwine.co.uk
01225 322800

Hailsham Cellars
www.hailshamcellars.com
01323 441212

Hamilton Yorke & Co
01258 820555

Hammerton Store
www.hammertonstore.co.uk
01224 324449

Handford Wines
www.handford.net
020 7221 9614

Hanging Ditch Wine Merchants
www.hangingditch.com
0161 832 8222

Harrods
www.harrods.com
020 7730 1234

Harvey Nichols
www.harveynichols.com
020 7235 5000

Hedley Wright Wine Merchants
www.hedleywright.co.uk
01279 465818

Hennings Wine Merchants
www.henningswine.co.uk
01798 872485

Hermitage Cellars
www.hermitagecellars.co.uk
01243 431002

Hic Wines
www.hic-winemerchants.com
01977 550047

Highbury Vintners
www.highburyvintners.co.uk
020 7226 1347

**HMWSA (Harvey-Miller
Wine and Spirit Agencies)**
www.hmwsa.com
0844 561 1252

Hoults Wine Merchants
www.hoults-winemerchants.co.uk
01484 510700

House of Fraser
www.houseoffraser.co.uk

The House of Menzies
www.houseofmenzies.com
01887 829666

Huntsworth Wine Co Ltd
www.huntsworthwine.co.uk
020 7229 1602

Imbibros
www.imbibros.co.uk
01252 723738

Indage (UK) Ltd
www.indagegroup.com
01536 446000

Jascots Wine Merchants
www.jascots.co.uk
020 8965 2000

J E Fells & Sons
www.fells.co.uk
01442 870900

Jeroboams & Laytons
www.jeroboams.co.uk
020 7288 8850

Latitude Wine & Liquor Merchant
www.latitudewine.co.uk
0113 245 3393

Lay & Wheeler
www.laywheeler.com
01473 313233

Le Pont de la Tour
020 7940 1840

Les Caves de Pyrene
www.lescaves.co.uk
01483 554750

Lewis & Cooper
www.lewisandcooper.co.uk
01609 772880

Liberty Wines
www.libertywine.co.uk
020 7720 5350

Luvians Bottleshop
www.luvians.com
01334 654820

**LVMH
(Moët Hennessy Louis Vuitton)**
www.lvmh.com
+33 1 4413 2222

Maison Marques & Domaines
www.mmdusa.net
020 8812 3380

Majestic Wine Warehouse
www.majestic.co.uk
0845 605 6767
(minimum purchase: 12 bottles)

Markinch Wine Gallery
01592 750024

Martinez Wines
www.martinez.co.uk
01943 600000

Mentzendorff
www.mentzendorff.co.uk
020 7840 3600

mollybrownswinelist.co.uk
www.mollybrownswinelist.co.uk
0845 604 0100

Morrisons
www.morrisons.co.uk
0845 611 6111

Negociants UK
www.negociantsuk.com
01582 462859

New Generation Wines
www.newgenerationwines.com
020 7403 9997

The New Zealand House of Wine
www.nzhouseofwine.co.uk
0800 085 6273

New Zealand Wine Distribution Co
www.nzwd.com

Noel Young Wines
www.nywines.co.uk
01223 844744

Novum
www.novumwines.com
020 7820 6720

Oddbins
www.oddbins.com
0800 917 4093

Oz Wines
www.ozwines.co.uk
0845 450 1261

Peckham & Rye
www.jwmunro.co.uk
0141 445 4339

Pernod Ricard UK
www.pernod-ricard-uk.com
020 8538 4484

Peter Lehmann UK
www.peterlehmannwines.com
01227 731 353

Philglas & Swiggot
www.philglas-swiggot.co.uk
020 8332 6031

Planet of the Grapes
www.planetofthegrapes.co.uk
020 7405 4912

PLB Group Ltd
www.plb.co.uk
01342 318282

Pol Roger UK
www.polroger.co.uk
01432 262800

Pure Wines
www.purewines.org
07790 282185

Quaff Fine Wine Merchant
www.quaffit.com
01273 820320

Quintessentially Wine
www.quintessentiallywine.com
0845 224 9261

Raeburn Fine Wines
www.raeburnfinewines.com
0131 332 5166

Redfield Wines
www.redfieldwines.co.uk
01803 845879

Revino
www.revino.co.uk
020 7349 8861

Rhythm & Booze
www.rhythmandbooze.co.uk
01226 215444

Richards Walford
www.r-w.co.uk

Sainsbury's
www.sainsburys.co.uk
0800 636 262

Seckford Wines
www.seckfordwines.co.uk
01394 446622

The Secret Cellar
www.thesecretcellar.co.uk
01892 537981

Selfridges & Co
www.selfridges.com
08708 377 377

Somerfield
www.somerfield.co.uk

Spar
www.spar.co.uk
020 8426 3700

Stevens Garnier
www.stevensgarnier.co.uk
01865 263300

The Sussex Wine Company
www.thesussexwinecompany.co.uk
01323 431143

Swig
www.swig.co.uk
0800 0 272 272

Tanners Wine Merchants
www.tanners-wines.co.uk
01743 234455

Tesco
www.tesco.com

Thierry's
www.thierrys.co.uk
01794 507 100

Thresher
www.threshergroup.com
01707 387200

Thorman Hunt & Co Ltd
020 7735 6511

Uncorked Wine Merchants
www.uncorked.co.uk
020 7638 5998

Unwined Ltd
www.unwined-online.co.uk
01949 844324

Valvona & Crolla
www.valvonacrolla.co.uk
0131 556 6066

Villeneuve Wines
www.villeneuvewines.com
01721 722500

The Vine Shop
www.thevineshop.co.uk
01920 485522

Vineyards : Sherborne
www.vineyards-sherborne.co.uk
01935 815544

Vinites
020 7924 4974

Vinology
www.vinology.co.uk
01789 264586

Vintage Roots
www.vintageroots.co.uk

Virgin Wines
www.virginwines.com
0870 164 9593

Waitrose
www.waitrose.com
0800 188 884

Weavers of Nottingham
www.weaverswines.com
0115 958 0922

Wheeler Cellars
www.wheelercellars.co.uk
01206 713560

White Vin Man
01580 712826

Whole Foods Market
www.wholefoodsmarket.com

Wildflower Wines
www.wildflowerwines.com
01506 844220

Wimbledon Wine Cellar
www.wimbledonwinecellar.com
020 8540 9979

Wine in Cornwall
www.wineincornwall.co.uk
01326 379426

Wine Rack
www.threshergroup.com
01707 387200

The Wine Society
www.thewinesociety.com
01438 740222

Wines of the World
www.winesoftheworld.co.uk
020 8947 7725

WoodWinters Wines & Whiskies
www.woodwinters.com
01786 834894

World Wine Agencies (Bath) Ltd
www.worldwineagencies.com
07764 372229

York Wines
www.yorkwines.co.uk
01347 878716

Ireland

64 Wine
www.64wine.com
+353 1 280 5664

Avoca Handweavers
+353 4 023 5105

Barry & Fitzwilliam Ltd
www.bandf.ie
+353 1 667 1755

Berry Bros & Rudd (Ireland)
www.bbr.com/ie.lml
+353 1 677 3444

Booze.ie
www.booze.ie
+353 1 289 1288

Bubble Brothers
www.bubblebrothers.com
+353 21 484 5198

Cabot & Co Fine Wines
www.cabotandco.com
+353 983 7000

Celtic Whiskey Shop
www.celticwhiskeyshop.com
+353 1 675 9744

The Corkscrew
www.thecorkscrew.ie
+353 1 674 5731

Direct Wine Shipments
www.directwineshipments.com
028 905 08000

Dunnes
www.dunnesstores.ie

Egan's Wines
www.eganwines.com
+353 65 708 1430

Fallon & Byrne
www.fallonandbyrne.com
+353 1 472 1010

Fine Wines
www.finewines.ie
+353 61 417 784

Gapwines
www.gapwines.com
028 90 781453

Harvest Off Licence
+353 9 179 2124

JJ Fox
www.jjfox.ie
+353 1 677 0533

James Nicholson Wine Merchant
www.jnwine.com
028 44830091

Jus De Vine
+353 1 846 1192

Karwig Wines
www.karwigwines.ie
+353 21 437 2864

Le Caveau
www.lecaveau.ie
+353 56 775 2166

Londis
www.londis.ie

Mary Pawle Wines
www.marypawlewines.com
+353 64 664 1443

McCabes Wines
www.mccabeswines.ie
+353 1 288 2037

Mill Wine Cellar
www.millwinecellar.ie
+353 1 6291022

Mitchell & Son Wine Merchant
www.mitchellandson.com
+353 1 2302301

Molloys Liquor Stores
www.molloys.ie
+353 1 451 5544

O'Briens
www.obrienswine.ie
+353 1 850 269 777

Oddbins (Ireland)
www.oddbins.com
+353 1 667 3033

O'Donovans Off Licence
www.odonovansofflicence.com
+353 21 429 6060

**Power & Smullen
Wine Merchant Ltd**
www.pswine.ie
+353 1 610 0362

Redmonds
www.redmonds.ie
+353 1 497 1739

Superquinn
www.superquinn.ie
+353 1 809 8500

Supervalu
www.supervalu.ie

Uncorked
www.uncorked.ie
+353 1 495 0000

Terroirs
www.terroirs.ie
+353 1 667 1311

The Vintry
www.vintry.ie
+353 1 490 5477

Wineonline.ie
www.wineonline.ie
+353 1 886 7732

Index of producers

Cheers!

This year's edition of **The Juice** would not have been possible without the help of the following individuals…

Matt Utber, Chris Terry, and all the crew at The Plant and Chris Terry Photography – massive love and respect to you all for once again helping to pull a huge rabbit out of a tiny hat. Also, massive thanks must go to the incredible John Corrigan for helping out hugely on the US edition. To Debbie Catchpole and Verity O'Brien at Fresh, and to Lisa Sullivan at Forum 5. Also, big thanks to my right-hand man Chris Franklyn. To all at Mitchell Beazley: Alison Goff, David Lamb, Leanne Bryan, Hilary Lumsden, Becca Spry, Fiona Smith, Pene Parker – and in the same breath, big thanks to Louise Sherwin-Stark and team at Hachette Australia. Thanks to Susanna Forbes. To my extended family: Jamie Oliver Inc and the Fifteen Group (London, Cornwall, Amsterdam, and Melbourne), Jonathan Downey and Match Group (London, Ibiza, New York, Chamonix, and Melbourne), Frank van Haandel, and Roger Fowler. Big shout-outs also to Judy Sarris at *Gourmet Traveller Wine*, Clare Patience at *Home Beautiful*, and Hamish McDougall at *GQ Australia* – thank you all for putting up with my lateness! To those behind the scenes; Mum, Drew, Caroline, Jessie, Eve, Anne, Thommo, Gin, Camilla, and Felix, Tobe and George, Randy, Pip and James, BP, CC and GG, Jamie and Jools, Ben Gillies and Chris Joannou, David Gleave, Philip Rich, Stuart Gregor, Cam Mackenzie, Andy Frost, The Jones, Cooper-Terry, and Utber clans, Lucas and Indigo at Odo for killer coffee, Dan Holland at Victoria Bitter, The Mighty Hawks, and beautiful Melbourne town.

M x

To find out more about our other great wine titles, join the Mitchell Beazley Wine Club

It's absolutely free to join and, as a member, you will receive:

- A newsletter containing sneak previews of our books together with news from our expert authors such as Hugh Johnson, Jancis Robinson, and, of course, Matt Skinner

- Advance notice of all our publications

- Members' discounts on our world-famous wine books

- Free entry to exclusive online competitions

To join, just follow the instructions at http://www.octopusbooks.co.uk/register

Remember, membership is FREE